Dr. Earl Mindell's
GARLIC
The Miracle Nutrient

Dr. Earl Mindell's

GARLIC
The Miracle Nutrient

Earl Mindell, R.Ph., Ph.D.

Keats Publishing, Inc.   New Canaan, Connecticut

DR. EARL MINDELL'S GARLIC: THE MIRACLE NUTRIENT

Copyright © 1994 by Earl L. Mindell, R.Ph., Ph.D.

All Rights Reserved

No part of this book may be reproduced in any form without the written consent of the publisher.

Library of Congress Cataloging-in-Publication Data

Mindell, Earl.
    Garlic : the miracle nutrient / Earl L. Mindell.
      p.   cm.
    Includes bibliographical references.
    ISBN 0-87983-649-0 : $4.95
    1. Garlic—Therapeutic use.   I. Title.
RM666.G15M54 1994
615'.324324—dc20   94-20651
                                       CIP

Printed in the United States of America

Published by Keats Publishing, Inc.
27 Pine Street, Box 876
New Canaan, Connecticut 06840-0876

Contents

Chapter One Garlic's 5,000-Year History 1

Two What's In It for Me? 11

Three What's Available 23

Four Garlic and Your Immune
System 38

Five Garlic and Your Heart.............53

Six Treating Cancer 73

Seven Cancer Prevention....................77

Eight Garlic, the "Germ" Fighter....93

Nine Garlic, Your Body's
Protector.................................107

Appendix A The First World Congress
on the Health Significance
of Garlic and Garlic
Constituents 120

Appendix B Garlic Colloquium/Europe
1991 127

Index..131

Dr. Earl Mindell's

GARLIC
The Miracle Nutrient

CHAPTER ONE
Garlic's 5,000-Year History

The "stinking rose" is featured in the Bible and in Homer's *Odyssey*. Aristotle, Hippocrates, Galen, Aristophanes, Virgil and Pliny were very familiar with this miracle healer for conditions which could fill a medical dictionary. Transylvanian peasants hung garlands of it over their windows and doorways to ward off vampires.

Until the turn of the century, no doctor's "black bag" would be without it. Albert Schweitzer used it at his clinic to treat an astounding variety of diseases. In World War I, battlefield physicians successfully prevented gangrene with poultices soaked in the juice of what later came to be called "Russian penicillin."

Still, it was relegated to folklore. Today, scientists are taking a serious look. In fact, in the past two decades, 2,000 studies conducted by the world's top researchers have established garlic's potential impact on the most serious modern diseases.

1

Best known throughout contemporary Western civilization for its distinctive and pungent flavor and odor, garlic is a hardy perennial bulb native to the Mediterranean regions of Europe and Africa. It was cultivated long before man began keeping written records, but many believe it originated in central Asia. Garlic is a member of the lily family, along with onions, chives, shallots, and leeks. Its botanical name, *Allium sativum*, may have its origins in the Celtic word *all*, which means "pungent."

The edible part of the garlic plant—the same part prized for its medicinal properties—grows beneath the ground and consists of a cluster of small cloves. Each clove is encased in a papery thin membranous envelope that separates it from the other cloves; the cloves are wrapped together into a bulb, which is also encased in layers of dry, papery membranes. Peeled and then chopped or minced, the cloves are used in cooking, and are also planted to generate new garlic crops.

Garlic cloves are dried in the field; they may then be eaten raw, but are often further dried and processed. While garlic is most often used as a spice or flavoring in cooking, it is also used as a nutritional supplement. The oil or juice may also be extracted and used in various garlic products. In fact, scientists today have even managed to separate the smell from the garlic in a supplement form, making it palatable for virtually everyone.

Garlic is rich in vitamin B1, a coenzyme in carbohydrate metabolism that keeps the nerves of the body healthy. Garlic also helps the body effectively absorb vitamin B1 because of *alli thiamine*, a conjugate of vitamin B1 and the S-allyl group (a group of chemical compounds characteristic to garlic). It also contains vitamin A and vitamin C, protein, and is a good source of a myriad of minerals, including calcium, magnesium, potassium, phosphorus, iron, copper, zinc, selenium, chloride, germanium, and sulfur compounds. Seventeen amino acids, including the eight manufactured by the body, can also be found in this valuable herb.

But the greatest nutritional benefit of garlic goes beyond the orthodox concept of nutrients—it lies in its components that can be utilized by the body in various ways. According to leading nutritionist and biophysicist Dr. Robert I. Lin, the most valuable of garlic's nutrients are the S-allyl compounds, such as S-allyl cysteine and S-allyl mercaptocysteine.

Aside from garlic and onions, few other foods contain significant amounts of these compounds, yet a number of studies have shown that these compounds are used by the body's cells for a variety of vital functions.

While garlic has traditionally been used as a spice or flavoring, it has also enjoyed a long history as a medicinal herb, used by peoples across the globe to treat and prevent a variety of conditions. Written accounts dating back 5,000 years mention garlic as both a food and a highly sought-after herbal remedy.

The first Biblical reference to garlic is in the Book of Numbers, when the Israelites following Moses into the wilderness reminisced about the abundance of food in their native Egypt, specifically, fish, cucumbers, melons, leeks, onions, and garlic. In the Talmud's Book of Ezra, Jews are encouraged to partake of garlic at the Friday night Shabbat.

The earliest written medical records contain detailed accounts of how garlic was used to prevent and treat disease. Garlic has been used medicinally for at least 4,000 years. It is mentioned more than twenty times in an ancient Egyptian medical papyrus called the Codex Ebers, dating to around 1550 B.C., which recommended it as a remedy for heart problems, tumors, headaches, worms, and bites. Indeed, the Egyptian pharaohs were entombed with carvings of garlic fashioned from either wood or clay.

Athletes at the first Olympic games in Greece were said to use garlic as a stimulant, and it was recommended by the founder of Islam, Mohammed. The Roman naturalist Pliny the Elder cited more than sixty therapeutic uses for this aromatic herb. Dioscorides, the chief physician to the Roman army during the first century A.D., prescribed garlic as an effective remedy for intestinal worms.

Garlic—often cooked, rarely raw—has been used in traditional Chinese medicine to treat conditions as diverse as angina pectoris, shigellosis, bronchitis, tuberculosis, appendicitis, malaria, boils, heart disease, tumors and various skin diseases. Interestingly, the Chinese traditionally aged whole clove garlic in vinegar for two or three years to enhance its medicinal properties. In India, it was used as an antiseptic lotion for washing wounds and healing ulcers.

The physician Galen, whose medical knowledge dominated the world for more than a thousand years, used garlic to treat a variety of illnesses and disorders. Perhaps the most intriguing stemmed from the tendency of political rivals to "defeat" their opponents by poisoning them. Galen used garlic as a successful antidote to most poisons used in that day.

In ancient times, garlic was also used by the Romans, Egyptians, Greeks and Israelites to ward off evil. Its use as a talisman persisted most among the Greeks. Greek midwives traditionally strung cloves of garlic around the birth room, and shouted "Garlic in your eyes!" to the newborn child to protect it from evil. Today, garlic is placed on piles of stones at crossroads, and its cloves are woven into garlands of wildflowers to ward off evil spirits.

Garlic was also believed by a number of cultures to have the power to ward off vampires. Transylvanian peasants draped garlands of it over their doorways to banish these fanged devils and evil spirits, and garlic cloves were hung around the necks of young girls throughout Europe to protect them from the vampire's deadly kiss. According to legend, the three things vampires feared the most were sunshine, the cross or crucifix and garlic. (It must work. Have you seen any vampires lately?)

During the Middle Ages, garlic was used throughout Europe to prevent the devastating bubonic plague. A dramatic example of the power of garlic occurred in England during the Great Plague of 1665, when the disease swept with a vengeance through the small town of Chester. The only residents of the entire town who were spared were those of God's Provident House, a storehouse whose cellars were filled with garlic. No one living in the house died.

When another plague spread through Europe in 1721, the French town of Marseilles was so badly hit that the surviving citizens dared not remove the bodies of those who had succumbed to the plague. They solved the problem by appointing four convicts condemned to death to deal with the bodies. Amazingly, the convicts survived—and retired on the loot they removed from the corpses. Their survival was credited to their drinking copious amounts of red wine in which garlic had been soaked. Today in Marseilles you can still purchase a similar garlic-laced "Four Thieves' Vinegar."

Later in the eighteenth century, garlic was used in Russia to successfully treat influenza. The American colonists used it for a variety of medicinal purposes, but valued it mainly for its ability to expel parasites. Later, Louis Pasteur studied it extensively and proclaimed in 1858 that it had antibacterial properties.

During the latter half of the nineteenth century, physicians throughout the world used garlic to treat a number of conditions, including typhus, cholera and whooping cough. An old wives' tale originating in the Middle Ages but current during the nineteenth century (and still practiced in some countries today) claimed garlic could cure whooping cough if rubbed on the soles of the child's feet. (Interestingly, garlic rubbed on the soles of the feet can be detected on the breath within ten minutes!)

Until the turn of the century, garlic was a staple carried by most physicians. It was used widely in both world wars, in hospitals and on the battlefield, to treat infection and prevent gangrene. The famous physician and humanitarian Albert Schweitzer used it in Africa to treat amoebic dysentery. Garlic later attained a status as a folk remedy, and was no longer taken seriously by scientists, medical practitioners or researchers until two decades ago, when garlic research blossomed in laboratories worldwide.

One research report on garlic concluded that the herb may have direct benefits against the "seven major diseases of our time"—hypertension (high blood pressure), hyperlipemia (high cholesterol), heavy metal intoxication, infectious diseases, free-radical damage, cancer and immune deficiency diseases.

Renewed interest in garlic as a powerful food supplement with potential medicinal properties has been a major factor in the development of the "Designer Foods Program," a five-year, $20.5-million program sponsored by the National Cancer Institute. This program is aimed at identifying foods that may prevent cancer.

"We're trying to develop new foods that will help prevent cells from becoming cancerous," explained Herbert F. Pierson, director of the program. He is spearheading intensive research on foods in five categories: garlic, linseed, licorice root, citrus fruit and members of the parsley family. The study hopes to develop "designer" foods—such as soups, cocktails, and even ice cream—that contain the specific cancer-preventive compounds that have been isolated from nature's pharmacy.

"Just consider the idea that there are substances in everyday foods that could prevent the expression of cancers, prevent blood clots, and prevent osteoporosis," Pierson said in an article published in *Eating Well.* "There is all this potential in our diet. We need to specifically focus the best components and fractions of edible plants into our food supply and diets."

The goals of the Designer Foods Program, according to Pierson, are to identify the phytochemicals in the specific foods that folklorists have touted for their healing abilities, and to then determine what effects those phytochemicals have on human health.

Once the most beneficial properties of the foods are identified, then scientists will go to work to "design" foods that will capitalize on these properties. As an example, Pierson noted, oranges contain ten different major phytochemicals that help reduce cholesterol, ease inflammation, and prevent certain kinds of cancer. The orange juice we normally drink contains the juice of only four oranges—and some of the most important phytochemicals are often eliminated during processing. In contrast, Pierson and his team may be able to come up with an orange juice that contains the essential phytochemicals of twenty oranges.

The U.S. Food and Drug Administration is eagerly anticipating the findings of the Designer Foods Program, and spokesman Chris Lecos told the *New York Times* that "There is a growing evidence that certain foods fight disease. We can no longer discourage the use of this information in labeling. We are looking at ways to regulate it."

Part of the mission of the Designer Foods Program, Pierson added, is to determine scientifically what has been bandied about in folklore for centuries—and to arrive at some sort of standardization. As an example, again he cites oranges, pointing out that every type of orange has its own unique phytochemical "fingerprint." Pierson and his research team hope to identify the exact species of each food that contains the maximum beneficial phytochemicals.

Of the six foods under Pierson's microscope, "Garlic is the one we're going after." Pointing out that garlic is most likely to have the greatest cancer preventive potential, Pierson said that "none of the other foods even comes close."

In determining maximum cancer preventive powers, scientists aimed at making a recommendation regarding the type of garlic th.

cultivated, the conditions under which it is grown, and the methods by which it is processed. After exhaustive research, the group settled on Kyolic Aged Garlic Extract, proclaiming it to be safe, effective, and of standardized quality. Subsequent Food and Drug Administration (FDA) investigations have found that the aged garlic extract has no potential adverse effects.

As research continues at the National Cancer Institute and other laboratories around the world, garlic is moving from the ranks of folklore to the forefront as a food with powerful medicinal qualities capable of strengthening the immune system, reducing the risk of heart disease, treating and preventing cancer, fighting infection and protecting against common environmental pollutants.

For more information on designer foods, see *Earl Mindell's Food as Medicine* (Simon and Schuster, 1994).

CHAPTER TWO
What's in It for Me?

The world, says State University of New York professor Eric Block, has always been divided into two camps: those who love garlic, and those who hate it. Chemists, he claims, are among those who love it—partly because "chemists have long been attracted to substances that have strong odors, sharp tastes, and marked physiological effects."

In reality, it was a pair of nineteenth-century German chemists, working separately, who laid the foundation for much of what we know today about the components of garlic and their medicinal values.

The first, Theodor Wertheim, noted in 1844 that there were small droplets of oil in the steam that rose when he boiled garlic. Using steam to further distill the garlic oil, he discovered pungent, volatile substances. He called the hydrocarbons in the oil *allyl* (derived from

11

the botanical *Allium*), a name that is still used today to describe the compounds that produce garlic's characteristic odor. He called the volatile substances in garlic oil *schwefelallyl,* or "allylsulfur" in English.

Following his discovery, Wertheim noted that garlic's appeal was due "mainly to the presence of a sulfur-containing, liquid body, the so-called garlic essential oil." He further noted that little was known about sulfur bonding, and challenged his fellow chemists to conduct the kind of study that would "supply useful results for science."

It was almost fifty years before another chemist took an in-depth look at the chemical constituents of garlic. In 1892 German researcher F. W. Semmler used the same method—steam distillation—to produce a highly concentrated, evil-smelling oil from raw cloves of garlic. Upon further investigation, Semmler discovered that the garlic oil yielded diallyl disulfide along with small amounts of diallyl trisulfide and other diallyl polysulfides.

Another fifty years passed before the next key discovery—this one by a team of American chemists—shed further light on the chemical components of garlic. In 1944, a group of researchers at New York's Sterling-Winthrop Chemical Company steeped garlic in ethyl alcohol at room temperature. The team, led by Chester J. Cavallito, found that steeping the garlic in alcohol—which was much less "vigorous" than steam distilling—resulted in a garlic oil that was both antibacterial and antifungal.

Cavallito named the chemically unstable, highly pungent, colorless liquid he produced *allicin*; this substance is what gives garlic its characteristic odor. Though allicin is the subject of a patent issued in the United States in Cavallito's name, its clinical use as an antibacterial agent was abandoned after only brief trials because of its instability.

Research conducted only four years later showed that allicin is not present in whole raw garlic; instead, allicin develops only after the garlic cells are "injured" (i.e., cut or crushed). As was reported in *Hippocrates*, "Despite its grand reputation, the garlic bulb itself looks humble—and is deceptively odorless. But crush one of the numerous cloves and you'll unleash dozens of volatile, biologically active sulfur compounds. The more finely chopped a garlic clove, the sharper its smell and taste. Or, as *The Official Garlic Lover's Handbook* puts it, 'The more you do to it, the more it will do to you.' "

Allicin is formed in part by a reaction of enzymes that starts when garlic is cut or crushed; other chemical reactions follow, resulting in the formation of a number of sulfur compounds. The important precursor of allicin, *alliin*, an odorless constituent of garlic, was discovered by chemists Arthur Stoll and Ewald Seebeck in 1948. Though some garlic manufacturers have recently tried to use alliin as a measure for standardizing garlic products, it is not useful as a measure; it is a starting material in raw garlic, not an end product in a manufactured commodity. Research conducted during the past four decades has shed further light on the chemical constituents of garlic and has led to the establishment of legitimate standards by which garlic products can be judged.

WATER-SOLUBLE COMPONENTS OF GARLIC

Researchers studying the chemical components of garlic have identified six major categories of water-soluble constituents. Since these are *water*-soluble, none are found in garlic oil.

Amino Acids (the building blocks of protein)

Probably the most important category of water-soluble components are the sulfur-containing amino acids derived from garlic. The sulfur-containing amino acids mainly include cysteine and its derivatives, including S-allyl cysteine, S-allyl mercaptocysteine, S-methyl cysteine, and gamma-glutamyl S-allyl cysteine.

Aggressive research conducted during the last ten years has shown that from a medical point of view, S-allyl cysteine is one of the most valuable constituents of garlic preparations. Odorless, stable, and safe, it has been shown to reduce levels of cholesterol in the blood, prevent clotting of the blood, protect the liver from toxic substances, and prevent chemically induced cancer in laboratory studies. A number of researchers have suggested the use of

S-allyl cysteine as a way of standardizing garlic products.

According to researchers, the water-soluble sulfur amino acids in garlic have been scientifically proven to be effective and safe. In addition, they have very little odor.

Enzymes (substances that either speed up or slow down a reaction)

Researchers have identified nine enzymes in garlic. All are composed of protein or protein and carbohydrate, all are water-soluble, and all are made inactive when heated. The most prevalent enzymes in garlic are peroxidase and alliinase. Garlic gets its characteristic odor from the enzymatic reactions. Alliinase acts on several specific sulfur compounds (particularly cysteine sulfoxide derivatives) in garlic; for example, it catalyzes the conversion of alliin (S-allyl-L-cysteine sulfoxide) to allicin.

Carbohydrates

Raw garlic has been found to contain seventeen different kinds of natural sugars. Of greatest importance may be the fructose-connected sugar fractions (called fructan or fructo-oligosaccharide) found in garlic; they contribute to the growth of *L. acidophilus* and *B. bifidum* (the "friendly" bacteria) in the intestinal tract, which promotes healthy digestion. Because these bacteria are destroyed by poor diet, antibiotics and other drugs, the use of garlic as a nutritional supplement may be especially beneficial.

Vitamins

Raw garlic contains five water-soluble vitamins: vitamin B1 (thiamine), vitamin B2 (riboflavin), vitamin C (ascorbic acid), nicotinic acid (niacin, or vitamin B3), and choline. These vitamins are essential for releasing energy from carbohydrates, proteins and fats; synthesizing nervous system chemicals; maintaining bones, teeth, capillaries and mucous membranes; and aiding in the formation of collagen, the body's main connective tissue.

Minerals

Scientists have identified nineteen minerals in garlic, including a number of essential macrominerals and trace minerals that have been shown to be important to human health.

The macrominerals identified in raw garlic include calcium, phosphorus, magnesium, potassium and sodium. They are essential for regulating body fluids, acids and bases; maintaining fluid and electrolyte balances in the body; releasing energy from carbohydrates, proteins and fats; conducting nerve impulses to the muscles; building bones and teeth and maintaining bone and muscle strength; and forming enzymes, cell membranes and genetic materials.

Trace minerals found in raw garlic include selenium, zinc, chromium, copper, iron, molybdenum, and manganese. They are vital for forming red blood cells; forming essential enzymes and proteins (zinc alone is part of more than 100 enzymes); enabling normal reproduction; promoting normal function of the nervous system; and preventing the breakdown of fats and other body chemicals.

Nucleosides or Nucleic Acids

Six kinds of nucleosides or nucleic acids—usually tied to the sugars or sugar derivatives in plants—are found in raw garlic. They include adenosine, guanosine, uridine, thymidine, cytidine and isosine. One of the most significant is adenosine, which plays an important role in human organic chemistry.

OIL-SOLUBLE COMPONENTS OF GARLIC

Garlic cloves do not contain oil-soluble, sulfur-containing compounds. However, once the cloves are crushed, oil-soluble compounds are produced through enzymatic reactions. As described earlier, garlic oil is manufactured through steam distillation. Simply put, crushed or ground raw garlic is submerged in water, which is then heated to distilling temperatures. Through the resulting distillation, the water and oil are separated. The oil is collected for processing; the water (including all the residues from the heated garlic) is discarded.

When the cloves are crushed, the alliin in the garlic converts to allicin; the allicin then decomposes at the high temperatures used during the distillation. The allicin decomposition products are the major components of garlic oil, which consists of diallyl disulfide, diallyl sulfide, diallyl trisulfide and small amounts of several other volatile sulfur compounds, including methyl allyl sulfide, dimethyl disulfide, methyl allyl disulfide and methyl allyl trisulfide. These oil-soluble compounds are highly volatile, extremely odorous and unstable.

THE CONFUSION SURROUNDING ALLICIN

Probably the most talked-about garlic compound among consumers is allicin—not because it is the most valuable, but because it is the most misunderstood. Some garlic manufacturers have relied heavily on allicin, focusing on that constituent as the key to garlic's medicinal value. Some have even promoted allicin as the best index for standardization among garlic products.

As mentioned earlier, raw garlic contains no allicin. What it *does* contain is alliin. When garlic cells are "injured," the enzyme alliinase converts alliin into allicin, a pungent, sulfur-containing compound. Garlic produces allicin to protect itself from bacteria and other disease-causing organisms.

According to Dr. Willis R. Brewer, dean and professor emeritus of the University of Arizona College of Pharmacy, allicin is extremely unstable and decomposes rapidly at room temperatures. With a half-life of little more than a few hours, most of the allicin in commercial garlic products is completely gone within a few weeks, even when vegetable or citrus oils are added as stabilizers. When the allicin content of leading brands of garlic products (including U.S. and German brands) was determined, none contained a detectable amount of allicin (less than one part per million). Garlic expert Dr. Robert I. Lin maintains that once allicin is formed, "it decomposes rapidly and is mostly lost within one day." Unless a garlic product is stored at extremely low temperatures, such as those obtained with liquid nitrogen, there is no way to stabilize allicin in the garlic product.

Since manufacturers have begun to realize that there is no allicin in any garlic supplement, they have started promoting "allicin potential" as a way of claiming their products can provide allicin to the body. "Allicin potential," however, is determined by adding water to the garlic product—a process that does not mimic what happens once the product is taken into the body. The production of allicin inside the body is very questionable.

Alliinase, the enzyme that causes the conversion of alliin to allicin, is irreversibly deactivated at the pH levels found in the human stomach. When garlic powder was incubated in simulated gastric fluid, only about 4 percent as much allicin was produced as when water was added. When the garlic powder was incubated in simulated intestinal fluid, only about 60 percent as much allicin was produced. When researchers *incubated subsequently in* simulated gastric and intestinal fluid, only about 1 percent as much allicin was produced as when the garlic powder was mixed with water. These recent findings demonstrate that only an insignificant amount of allicin can be produced inside the body.

Even *if* some allicin is delivered to the digestive tract, recent studies have shown that it is not bioavailable—in other words, it is not in a form that can be used by the body. Allicin reacts quickly with the blood and oxidizes it. When allicin is mixed with blood, all the allicin disappears within a few minutes, and the color of the blood turns from red to black. The allicin oxidizes the hemoglobin in the red blood cells to methemoglobin—a substance that can't carry oxygen to the organs and tissues.

Because all nutrients or substances taken by mouth and absorbed by the intestine must first go through the liver, researchers have studied how allicin reacts in the liver. Only allicin in a high-enough concentration to cause severe liver cell damage can be detected after it passes through the liver. Allicin disappears very rapidly when incubated with liver homogenate.

Other studies have shown that even after eating 25 grams of raw garlic—which contains a *significant* amount of allicin—no allicin could be detected in either the blood or the urine from one to twenty-four hours later.

Researchers have concluded, then, that allicin is *not* "bioavailable"—cannot be used by the body—and does not seem to be the biologically active compound of garlic.

Not only is allicin nonbioavailable and unstable, but there's another problem, too: The oxidative and cell-killing effects of allicin don't discriminate; they damage all kinds of cells, including "friendly" and non-disease-causing cells. Some of the known effects of allicin are oxidation of red blood cells, damage to liver cells (like that mentioned above), inflammation of the stomach, and hemolytic anemia.

Toxicity is an issue of utmost importance when choosing a garlic product or other food supplement to take daily on a long-term basis. Garlic has been safely used as a popular condiment or flavoring and has been used traditionally for medicinal purposes. But *raw garlic*, on the other hand, can cause a variety of adverse effects in large amounts. Common ill effects of large doses of raw garlic are burning sensations and diarrhea. Scientific publications from 1932 to 1993 have reported six verified toxic effects of large doses of raw garlic preparations:

- Stomach disorders and diarrhea
- Decreases in protein and calcium levels in the bloodstream
- Anemia
- Bronchial asthma
- Contact dermatitis (burning or skin rashes on contact)
- Decreased fertility (due to inhibition of sperm)

In addressing members of the First World Congress on the Health Significance of Garlic and Garlic Constituents (Appendix A), Dr. Lin, who chaired the Congress, summed up the controversy over allicin by saying that the "claim that allicin is the only active principle of garlic is unfounded; rather, it has little direct contribution to garlic's nutritional and pharmacological properties."

CHAPTER THREE
What's Available

The recent frenzy of garlic research has spawned a generation of consumers who are eager to try garlic for its health benefits—but who are confounded when confronted with an astonishing array of commercial garlic products on the market. Which garlic product to try, or whether to favor a raw clove over a commercially bottled product, has become a source of concern for garlic consumers worldwide.

Commercial manufacturers and their marketing teams have what seems like an endless array of options in what is on the marketplace: Since garlic oil was first isolated in 1844, more than 100 compounds have been identified as constituents of garlic. Attempts have been made to isolate one or two of these, to attribute specific medical claims to each, and to launch a marketing effort based on those compounds.

Continuing scientific research has fed, rather than discouraged, these kinds of commercial tactics. As new compounds (such as ajoene) are discovered and scientifically tested, garlic manufacturers rush to the forefront to be the first to include information and claims about those compounds. In some cases, product manufacturers tout compounds or constituents that have not even been fully proven to exist by teams of independent scientists.

And recently, some garlic manufacturers have promoted the concept of standardized garlic based on chemical composition. Many have suggested the use of allicin or allicin-producing potential as the means for standardization—even though, as detailed in Chapter Two, allicin is not a desirable end product nor is it stable enough to be measured in commercial products on the market.

There are myriad difficulties with the concept of standardizing garlic products. According to nutritionist and biophysicist Dr. Robert I. Lin, "From a nutritional and pharmacological point of view, standardization of herbs by chemical indices should not be done haphazardly. In order to achieve such standardization, the beneficial properties, the toxicity aspects, and the active principles of an herb must be well-understood, well-defined and/or well-characterized. Without such knowledge, a haphazard standard may be established that would imply a guaranteed potency or benefit."

The obvious problem that follows, says Dr.

Lin, is that "such an implied potency or benefit may mislead consumers to falsely depend on a product that cannot deliver upon its implied promises."

Still another challenge in standardization, Dr. Lin adds, is that the active principle that is used as an index for standardization must be stable throughout normal processing, marketing, and distribution. If it isn't, he points out, "by the time the product is used, the active principle would have decomposed."

The challenge of standardizing garlic is particularly complex, partly because garlic itself has extremely complex chemical, pharmacological, and nutritional properties. A first step in standardization is to determine which beneficial effects of garlic should be used for standardization—and the obvious follow-up is to identify exactly which substances in garlic contribute to those effects.

Both steps are unrealistic at this time. First, there is widespread disagreement about which beneficial effect of garlic should be used as a standard—some want to use the germicidal properties of garlic, which enable it to kill microorganisms, while other scientists prefer to concentrate on garlic's effectiveness in lowering cholesterol, preventing cancer, reducing blood pressure or enhancing the immune system. Even when a benefit is generally agreed on, it would be difficult at this time, despite aggressive and ongoing research by teams of scientists throughout the world, to determine exactly which constituent of garlic is responsible.

Though there is difficulty of standardization, the consumer has four basic choices regarding garlic products: the whole-clove garlic, which includes fresh garlic juice and cooked garlic; dehydrated garlic powders made by drying clove garlic; garlic oils made by distilling garlic extracts and diluting them with vegetable oils; and aged garlic extract, in which organically grown garlic is aged to gently convert the harsh and unstable compounds found in raw garlic to stable, safe and beneficial odorless compounds.

RAW GARLIC, FRESH JUICE, AND COOKED GARLIC

With all garlic's proven medicinal values, consumers undoubtedly are tempted to reach for the easiest and most convenient garlic product of all: a raw clove of garlic. As detailed in Chapter Two, however, as soon as the garlic cells are cut or crushed, a rapid chemical process begins that converts alliin into allicin, the sulfur compound that gives fresh raw garlic its distinctive odor. Allicin is also the compound that gives raw garlic its toxicity.

Allicin is a powerful oxidant with strong cytocidal power, which means that it has the ability to kill cells. That cytocidal power is what promoted the "allicin hysteria" of four or five decades ago, when researchers looking for compounds with antibiotic power turned to allicin as a powerful germ-killing agent. However, research found that allicin lacked the

26

ability to distinguish between harmful cells and beneficial cells—it simply killed them all, including cells of the human body.

When raw garlic is cut or crushed, the conversion to allicin is immediate and compelling. Unfortunately, other chemical conversions require time and controlled conditions, so raw garlic ends up doing harm as well as good—a fact that has been proven scientifically. Garlic researchers have proven that raw garlic, at doses high enough to be effective medicinally, can cause burns and inflammation of the mucous membranes lining the mouth, throat, and stomach. It can also damage red blood cells, causing a form of anemia, destroy the friendly bacteria in the intestinal tract, and inhibit the intestines from absorbing the nutrients from food, and interfere with liver function.

The first link between large intake of raw garlic and one of its well-known side effects— anemia, or damage to red blood cells—was discovered accidentally, as so often happens in medical research. Early in this century, physicians practicing in sanitariums gave tuberculosis patients raw garlic juice in the belief that is antibiotic properties would destroy the bacteria that caused the disease.

Physicians who began giving patients more garlic as a nutritional supplement in an attempt to better contro! the tuberculosis noticed that the patients became anemic. As reported in *Experimental Medicine* in 1932, a professor of medicine in Japan made the connection between the raw garlic supplements and the anemia. The proof then became obvious when the physicians stopped giving the patients raw garlic and the anemia cleared up.

Subsequent scientific studies performed during the next few years and reported in *Clinical Pathology and Hematology*, established a clear link between raw garlic and anemia. Today's researchers point out that, although normal amounts of raw garlic normally used to season food rarely cause anemia, daily supplementation with large doses of raw garlic could cause this blood disorder.

As research advanced, scientists discovered other toxic side effects of raw garlic. The results of a variety of studies show that raw garlic damages the sensitive mucous membranes lining the gastrointestinal tract. In one study, which was reported in *The Journal of Toxicological Sciences*, healthy rats were fed raw garlic and then examined. Researchers found that the garlic had caused extensive damage to the rats' stomachs, including swelling, ulceration, and massive bleeding. Among the most common side effects of eating raw garlic are nausea, vomiting, and diarrhea.

(It's easy to visualize what raw garlic does to the mucous membranes of the mouth, throat, and stomach. Simply rub a sliced clove of raw garlic on your skin—the toxic irritants in the garlic cause the skin to turn red.)

Cooking totally changes the chemical composition of the sulfur-containing compounds in garlic. During cooking, the allicin (which is produced when the raw garlic is sliced or ground) decomposes into a number of other odorous sulfur-containing compounds, including diallyl sulfide, diallyl disulfide and diallyl trisulfide. These compounds are so volatile that they are partially lost; you may have noticed that cooked garlic has less odor than raw garlic. Cooking generally removes most of garlic's toxicity through the chemical conversion of sulfur-containing compounds, but the benefits of cooked garlic vary substantially, depending on the cooking conditions—such as temperature, duration of the cooking period, and other ingredients the garlic was cooked with. Different methods of cooking garlic, therefore, result in inconsistent health benefits.

DEHYDRATED GARLIC POWDERS

Garlic powder is prepared by dehydrating garlic cloves, then grinding them into powder. Because garlic is 60 to 70 percent water, manufacturers claim that 1 gram of garlic powder is equivalent to 2.5 to 3.3 grams of raw garlic. But if you consider chemical composition, garlic powder is not simply dried-up garlic. Here's a good example: raw garlic is about 1 percent alliin. Theoretically, then, dehydrated garlic would be 2.5 to 3.3 percent alliin. That's not what happens, though. The alliin content of commercial garlic powder is less than half what you'd expect using the above formula—which indicates that more than half the alliin in raw garlic is lost during the manufacturing process. So even though garlic powder may contain most of the same constituents as raw garlic, they exist in different amounts—some higher, some lower—in garlic powder.

Garlic powder contains some alliin and alliinase, and produces some amount of allicin with the addition of water. Therefore, manufacturers of garlic powder strongly promote allicin and/or allicin production potential in their products. However, the truth is that no garlic powder contains a detectable amount of allicin, and the production of allicin inside the body is very questionable. On the other hand, the production of allicin inside the body could be dangerous due to the following reasons: allicin causes undesirable effects, including the oxidation of essential body components and killing of the body cells, and the production of another toxic substance, ammonia, accompanies the enzymatic production of allicin.

GARLIC OIL

Garlic oil is manufactured by distilling raw garlic, isolating its essential oil, and diluting the oil with vegetable oil (such as soybean oil). It's necessary to dilute garlic oil; it is highly odorous and toxic because of the organic sulfides found in pure garlic oil, such as diallyl disulfide, methyl allyl trisulfide and diallyl trisulfide.

It takes 500 milligrams of raw garlic to produce 1 to 2 mg of garlic essential oil. The constituents of garlic essential oil do have some health benefits (such as reducing blood clotting and preventing cancer), but most commercial garlic products are diluted 100 times by vegetable oil to overcome the odor and toxicity problems. As a result, an average capsule of commercial garlic essential oil actually contains less than one drop of garlic oil. Most of what the consumer pays for is vegetable oil.

That's not all. High temperatures are used to distill the volatile oil-soluble compounds in garlic. The garlic oil that results, then, does not contain any nonvolatile components including vitamins, minerals, enzymes, and amino acids that make garlic such a valuable nutritional supplement.

To sum it up, garlic oil contains only a small fraction of garlic—so it provides only a small fraction of garlic's benefits. The water-soluble compounds, the most beneficial compounds in garlic, are missing from garlic oil. Because of the very process by which it is manufactured, garlic oil *can't* represent all the nutrients and compounds found in a raw clove of garlic.

AGED GARLIC EXTRACT

Throughout history, garlic has traditionally been aged in wine, vinegar, or some other media to reduce toxicity and enhance its beneficial properties. Ancient Chinese textbooks describe a method of aging garlic for two to three years before the herb was used for medicinal purposes. The popular French "Four Thieves' Vinegar" still marketed in Marseilles represents the red wine in which garlic had been steeped that protected convicts against the plague during the Middle Ages.

The modern processing method of manufacturing aged garlic extract had its beginnings in the 1950s, when Dr. Eugene Schnell, a former professor of medicinal chemistry at Berlin University and then an administrative chief with the Japanese Drug Administration, joined forces with Manji Wakunaga to develop Kyolic Aged Garlic Extract. In 1991, Wakunaga was given the Ministry of Science and Technology Award—the highest recognition given by the Japanese government to an individual—for his role in developing Kyolic.

The unique natural cold-aging process used to manufacture the extract has attracted recent international attention because it results in a product shown to be both safe and effective by researchers, including those of the United States Food and Drug Administration. The success of the natural cold-aging process begins with what happens to garlic once it is cut or crushed. As State University of New York researcher Eric Block told *National Geographic,* "Undisturbed, the garlic bulb has limited medicinally active compounds. Cutting triggers the formation of a cascade of compounds that are quite reactive and participate in a complex sequence of chemical reactions. Ultimately, an amazing collection of chemical compounds is produced."

According to research reported by *National Geographic,* garlic unleashes at least 100 sulfur-containing compounds—sulfur compounds that are linked to its therapeutic value. The process by which a garlic supplement is manufactured determines whether those sulfur-containing compounds are preserved for optimal medicinal value.

Most garlic manufacturers fail to recognize that potentially hundreds of sulfur compounds can increase a garlic supplement's effectiveness. Instead, they make claims about the amount of alliin in their products, or their product's allicin-producing potential. But alliin is the starting point for a variety of sulfur-containing compounds; a garlic supplement that contains alliin—regardless of whether it contains alliinase—won't necessarily result in the formation of important sulfur-containing compounds inside the body. Even if some occur, they can't be controlled—so there's no guarantee that the important compounds will be formed.

The transformation of garlic's active components makes clear the difference between traditional methods of manufacture and the natural cold-aging used to produce Kyolic Aged Garlic Extract. To begin with, an intact garlic cell contains certain enzymes, peptides, and amino acids, including alliin, an odorless sulfur-containing amino acid. When garlic is cut or crushed, the resulting chemical reactions convert alliin into allicin. Allicin, which is highly unstable, rapidly decomposes under uncontrollable chemical reactions to produce a variety of oil-soluble organosulfur compounds, including diallyl sulfide, diallyl disulfide, diallyl trisulfide, and ajoene. Because these chemical reactions are uncontrollable, the content of the sulfur-containing compounds varies from one batch to another.

In the cold-aging process used to manufacture the Kyolic extract, on the other hand, the raw garlic is carefully sliced and placed in a extracting solution in large stainless steel tanks, where it is naturally cold-aged for up to twenty months without using heat.

During the natural cold-aging process, the allicin decomposes and certain compounds are bioconverted. These combined effects lead to several oil-soluble organosulfur compounds and a great number of water-soluble organosulfur compounds that are safe and stable—resulting in an effective, odorless product.

As the aging process begins, the sliced garlic cloves produce small amounts of allicin, which are gradually converted to a variety of oil-soluble sulfur-containing compounds. But that's only part of the aging process. The important distinction is that the natural bioconversion process that takes place during aging results in the ideal conversion of raw garlic's constituents into numerous effective, safe, and stable water-soluble organosulfur compounds, including S-allyl cysteine (SAC). Kyolic is the first garlic supplement to offer standardized levels of SAC, and both Aged Garlic Extract and S-allyl cysteine are protected by more than twelve international patents and patents pending.

The safety and effectiveness of Kyolic Aged Garlic Extract has led to its wide acceptance among the scientific community. Many of the research projects examining the properties of garlic have relied on it because of its stability, effectiveness and absence of toxic side effects. Fourteen of the abstracts reported at the First World Congress held in Washington, D.C. in 1991 (see Appendix A) were presented by scientists who used the product exclusively in their research.

The Quality of Garlic Bulbs Used in Garlic Products

Because garlic is an agricultural product, its quality varies and depends on the cultivating conditions, such as climate, soil condition, and treatment with fertilizers and pesticides. Most desirable is garlic that is organically cultivated. To obtain the kind of uniform quality garlic needed in the manufacture of herbal medicines and food supplements, garlic cultivation must be stringently controlled from seed to harvest. Only those garlic bulbs that meet the most stringent specifications are suitable for use in daily supplement products—but most garlic products are made from conventional bulbs. Only Kyolic Aged Garlic Extract is made from organically grown garlic that meets predetermined specifications, including freedom from contaminants and suitable content of protein, sugar, and certain sulfur-containing compounds.

The Toxicity of Raw versus Aged

One of the greatest benefits of natural cold-aging is the safety of the garlic product. According to leading garlic researcher and biophysicist Dr. Robert Lin, ingestion of 3 grams of commercial garlic powder causes burning sensations, irritation, indigestion, loss of appetite, and diarrhea. The use of Kyolic extract does not cause these side effects, nor any other side effects.

Sophisticated scientific testing confirms the safety of aged garlic extract over raw garlic. In one Japanese study, which was published in *The Journal of Toxicological Sciences*, researchers divided healthy rats into three groups. The first group was fed raw garlic juice; the second group was fed the extract; and the third group, which was used as a control, was fed distilled water.

Researchers noticed almost immediate changes in the rats that were fed raw garlic juice. Almost immediately after feeding on the raw garlic juice, *every* rat experienced lacrimation, decreased mobility, and a slight walking disturbance. Researchers also noted that body hairs were standing up on all the rats that were fed the raw garlic juice. These symptoms were not noted in rats that received aged garlic extract.

Five of the rats who were fed raw garlic juice at high dosages died during the first fifteen days of the test. On autopsy, researchers found that the cause of death was massive bleeding in the stomach.

All of the rats who were fed raw garlic juice suffered from gastric bleeding, retardation of growth, diarrhea, swelling of the liver, and a decrease in the size of the spleen and lymph glands (suggesting a compromised immune system). None of these effects were suffered by the rats who were fed aged garlic extract or distilled water.

Other sophisticated tests have shown that raw garlic oxidizes red blood cells and results in the formation of methemoglobin, a substance that can't carry oxygen. Scientists have examined vials of human red blood-cell contents to which raw garlic juice or garlic extract has been added. Adding raw garlic juice causes the blood to turn black, but adding the extract does not cause any darkening of the red blood cells.

In additional sophisticated tests, scientists have shown that aged garlic extract even protects human red blood cells against the effects of a mild oxidant (t-butylhydroperoxide) added to the human red blood-cell suspension.

CHAPTER FOUR
Garlic and Your Immune System

Your immune system is your body's main line of defense, not only against minor irritations such as the common cold, but against life-threatening diseases such as cancer. In fact, a healthy immune system features a powerful "surveillance" system that seeks out and destroys defective or mutinous cells, such as cancer cells.

When your immune system is compromised, your body is not as adept at fighting off invading organisms; your body becomes susceptible to a variety of bacterial, fungal, and viral diseases. Cancer cells are no longer held in check, and tumors can develop. If your immune system is completely inactivated (which happens in immune deficiency diseases, such as acquired immune deficiency syndrome or AIDS), your body is unable to fight off invading organisms.

Immunity can be compromised by poor diet, environmental pollution, stress, disease, abnormalities at birth, and even the natural process of aging. Fortunately, science has identified some things that stimulate the immune system, and one of them is garlic. Garlic is rich in sulfur-containing amino acids and contains elements that may promote activity of the immune system's cells, especially the macrophages and the natural killer cells. Garlic may have such a powerful effect, according to an article in *The Journal of the National Medical Association*, that it "may become known as one of the grand conductors of the body's immune symphony."

To understand how garlic enhances immunity, here is how your immune system works. There are five major categories of immune cells: the B lymphocytes, the T lymphocytes, the phagocytes, the killer cells, and the natural killer cells.

The B lymphocytes have the ability to recognize "foreign" substances or invaders; the B lymphocytes produce antibodies in response to these foreign invaders. The antibodies attack and bind to the invading substances, finally inactivating or destroying them. Once manufactured, the antibodies have the ability to consistently recognize and destroy those specific invaders; this principle is what makes it possible for immunizations and vaccinations to protect against disease. When the body is first invaded by a foreign substance, the production of antibodies takes quite a long time, so it is possible for the invader to cause serious illness, and even death. But once B lymphocytes memorize a foreign substance, they are then able to produce antibodies as soon as the invader is recognized, preventing illness and death.

For example, a tiny amount of polio virus is introduced into your body with the polio vaccine. The B lymphocytes recognize the polio virus as a foreign substance, and start producing antibodies that destroy the virus. Any subsequent polio virus that later enters your body will be destroyed by these same antibodies, which are permanently programmed to destroy the polio virus.

It is through this same principle that some diseases—such as chicken pox, mumps, infectious mononucleosis and respiratory syncytial virus—cannot infect the same person more than once.

The remaining categories of immune system cells—the T lymphocytes, phagocytes, killer cells and natural killer cells—respond by directly attacking the invaders. These are the cells, for example, that launch a direct attack on cancer cells, streptococcal bacteria, and other disease organisms. T lymphocytes also produce a variety of chemicals called *lymphokines* that control or modulate the immune system through either stimulation or suppression.

IMMUNE-ENHANCING EFFECTS OF GARLIC

A recent variety of studies involving garlic and the immune system show that garlic is effective in enhancing overall immune function as well as strengthening and empowering the individual cells of the immune system. These findings could help clarify the mechanism through which traditional garlic use has been effective against infectious diseases.

Natural Killer Cells

Recent studies have confirmed that garlic stimulates the ability of natural killer cells to destroy tumor cells, virus-infected cells, and foreign invaders.

In one dramatic study reported in the *Journal of Urology*, researchers first implanted mice with a cell line derived from murine transitional cell carcinoma, a particularly virile form of bladder cancer characterized by aggressive growth. They then treated the mice with varying doses of aged garlic extract.

Researchers then examined the mice to determine both the size of the tumor masses and the infiltration of natural killer cells that could destroy the cancer cells in the tumor. They found that both the reduction in tumor mass and the increase in infiltration of natural killer cells that destroyed the cancer cells depended on the dose: the higher the dose of garlic the mice were given, the better the mice were able to fight the cancer.

A landmark experiment conducted by Florida pathologist Tariq Abdullah tested the effect of garlic on natural killer cells. In his study, which was reported to the Federation of American Societies for Experimental Biology in

1989, Dr. Abdullah randomly divided volunteers into three groups. Over a three-week period, one group took raw garlic, one group took Kyolic Aged Garlic Extract, and the third group (the control group) took no garlic at all. Blood samples were taken from each volunteer before the study began and again three weeks later; Dr. Abdullah and his colleagues tested natural killer cells in the blood against tumor cells in test tubes.

Before the test began, the natural killer-cell activity of volunteers in all three groups were basically similar. But the differences after taking garlic for three weeks were staggering: the natural killer cells of those who took raw garlic killed 140 percent more tumor cells than those of the control group. And the natural killer cells of those who took the extract killed *160 percent more tumor cells* than those in the control group.

In commenting on the results of the study, Dr. Abdullah pointed out that use of garlic— even for a period as brief as three weeks—will stimulate natural killer cells and will exert an immunopotentiating effect on the entire immune system. In a report of the study published in the *Journal of the National Medical Association*, Dr. Abdullah added that the findings "suggest that garlic may have an effect on other components of cell-mediated immunity, including macrophages and T-cells."

The stimulation of natural killer cell activity by aged garlic extract has recently been confirmed by *in vitro* tests. Dr. Reiko Irie, a former

UCLA professor now at California's John Wayne Cancer Institute, and her colleagues prepared lymphocytes from human blood. The lymphocytes were mixed with aged garlic extract and its fractions, and were then incubated for a certain period of time. Treatment with the extract significantly increased the natural killer cell activity when compared to the control lymphocytes that were incubated in the plain medium.

Interestingly, the effect of the garlic is at least partially dependent on how it is administered. Dr. Benjamin Lau of California's Loma Linda University School of Medicine carried his research using the mice a step further to determine which method of treatment was most effective. Some of the mice with murine transitional cell carcinoma were given injections of garlic extract in the peritoneal cavity. Other mice received injections directly into the tumors.

Dr. Lau and his researchers discovered that injection directly into the tumors was much more effective in arresting the cancer: such injections resulted in almost "complete inhibition of tumor growth," according to a report of the study published in *Molecular Biothermal Science.* The intraperitoneal injections of garlic extract, in contrast, resulted in only "partial"—though still significant—inhibition of tumor growth.

Macrophages

Macrophages are a type of phagocyte that engulf or "phagocytize" foreign substances, including microorganisms, and that play a primary role in immune function.

In an initial study conducted in Japan and reported in *Phytotherapy Research* in 1987, researchers first proved that aged garlic extract and its fractions stimulated the activity of macrophages in a test tube. The same kind of immune activity stimulation was then shown in animals: healthy mice were given the extract, then carbon particles (representing foreign substances) were injected intravenously. Researchers monitored how quickly the mice cleared the carbon particles from their blood. The mice that received the extract cleared the carbon particles in the blood more quickly than the control mice who did not. Since phagocytic cells (including macrophages and the cells in the spleen and lymph nodes) can clear carbon particles in the blood, researchers concluded that aged garlic extract made the carbon particles clear more quickly by stimulating the phagocytes.

Following that initial study, Dr. Lau and his colleagues at Loma Linda University School of Medicine did three studies to examine in more detail how garlic stimulates macrophage activity. For the test, they used a measurement of activity called *chemiluminescence*, a gauge of how much light the cells emit. The greater the fighting ability of the macrophages, the more light they emit.

For the first study, reported in *The International Clinical Nutrition Review*, Dr. Lau and his colleagues used three groups of mice. The first group of mice received liquid Kyolic Aged Garlic Extract in the groin. The second group of mice received the same preparation injected into the peritoneal cavity. The third group of mice did not receive any garlic at all, and acted as controls.

Four days after the researchers injected the mice, they examined macrophages and other immune cells from the peritoneal cavity, the spleen and the inguinal lymph nodes of each mouse. They used chemiluminescence to determine how potent the immune cells were and how well they could engulf and destroy foreign particles.

When compared to the mice that received no garlic at all, the mice who received garlic injections in the groin showed only a slight increase in phagocytic activity of macrophages in the peritoneal cavity or the spleen. However, they showed "significantly greater" activity in the inguinal lymph nodes, which lie in the groin.

When compared to the mice that received no garlic, the mice who received garlic injections in the peritoneal cavity showed better phagocytic activity in the inguinal lymph nodes. But the differences in activity of macrophages in the peritoneal cavity and the spleen were staggering.

In commenting on the study, Dr. Lau said that research results show that "if the disease is localized, a localized treatment should be given, whereas systemic disease should be treated with a systemic treatment." In other words, Dr. Lau cautioned, "systemic therapy shouldn't always be the automatic choice of treatment."

Dr. Lau expanded the concept of his study to include that of a "triangle," pointing out that all three factors must be present before infection or disease can occur. The triangle of disease includes a compromised status in the *host*, such as weakened immunity, poor nutrition, or an at-risk lifestyle; *predisposing factors*, such as trauma, toxic exposure, stress, or underlying disease; and, finally, the *microbes* that cause the disease.

Dr. Lau remarked that "scientific research seems to support the ancient belief in the medical benefits of garlic." In addition, he said, garlic appears to have touched on all three aspects of the triangle: the ability to inhibit the growth of microbes (including certain cancer cells), the ability to enhance the host's resistance to disease, and the ability to protect the host from toxic exposures. (For more information on the ability of garlic to protect against environmental pollutants and free radicals, see Chapter Nine.)

In a second study, Dr. Lau and his colleagues examined the effectiveness of liquid Kyolic Aged Garlic Extract on systemic fungal infection. They intravenously injected *Candida albicans*, a disease-causing yeast organism, into mice. After randomly dividing the mice into two groups, researchers gave one group intraperitoneal injections of the extract, the other group (the controls) saline injections. Researchers then measured the Candida in the blood and kidney at 24-hour intervals.

Twenty-four hours after the yeast was injected, researchers found 3,500 colonies of Candida in the blood of the control mice but only 400 colonies in the mice that had been treated with the garlic extract. After 48 hours, there were no Candida colonies in the blood of these mice, but there were still 1,400 colonies in the control mice. Observation of the colonization of Candida in the kidneys of the mice at 24-hour intervals showed significantly lower numbers in the group treated with the extract.

In the same study, researchers noticed stimulated phagocytic activity of the macrophages among the mice treated with Kyolic. The researchers concluded that the control of the Candida infection might have been mediated through the enhanced phagocytic function of the treated mice.

In the third study, Dr. Lau and his colleague, Dr. Yamasaki, tested the fighting ability of macrophages after they were exposed to one of four commercial garlic preparations. Using chemiluminescence, they found that the Kyolic product significantly enhanced the fighting ability of macrophages. One other preparation was slightly effective at low doses, but proved to be too toxic at higher doses. The other two commercial garlic preparations showed very little ability to boost the fighting ability of the macrophages.

Based on his research and the review of a

number of other scientific studies, Dr. Lau is convinced of the effectiveness of garlic against infectious diseases. In the past, researchers thought garlic was effective against infectious diseases because of direct antifungal activity, mainly by allicin. But since allicin is not bioavailable, it is not active inside the body—and it can't be the key to garlic's effectiveness against infectious disease. Instead, garlic appears to stimulate macrophages and lymphocytes to attack the disease-causing organism. After testing a number of commercial garlic preparations, Dr. Lau found that Kyolic Aged Garlic Extract significantly enhances the fighting ability of macrophages, while other garlic preparations seem to have only a marginal effect. Its effectiveness, says Dr. Lau, is probably due to the compounds converted during the cold-aging process.

OTHER IMMUNE FUNCTIONS

Lymphokine-Activated Killer Cell (LAK) Activity

Recent successful studies have identified several lymphokines that can enhance or suppress immune functions. Interleukin (IL) II, a type of lymphokine, enhances the ability of T lymphocytes to kill tumor cells. Generally, peripheral T lymphocytes cannot destroy tumor cells; however, when they are mixed with IL-II, they acquire killer cell activity. This is referred to as *lymphokine-activated killer cell activity*. Dr.

Reiko Irie's group reported in *Cancer Immunology Immunotherapy* that aged garlic extract enhanced IL-II activity. When cells are incubated with both IL-II and a water-soluble fraction of aged garlic extract, the T lymphocytes were able to kill even more tumor cells. In other words, the same dose of IL-II, when mixed with aged garlic extract, changed more T cells to killer cells.

Proliferation of Lymphocytes

Lymphocytes multiply slowly unless they are stimulated. Although aged garlic extract itself doesn't significantly stimulate the lymphocytes, it *does* enhance their proliferation in response to the mitogens Con A and PHA. This observation indicates that aged garlic extract stimulates immune function by influencing the way T lymphocytes respond to lymphokines and mitogens.

Stress and the Immune System

The immune system can be compromised by many factors, among them stress, poor diet, and environmental pollution. In one study conducted in Japan, the production of immunoglobulin was decreased by stress (restrained stress) in mice. When mice were given aged garlic extract before they were exposed to stress, their immune system suffered less inhibition.

GARLIC AND AIDS RESEARCH

Based on his landmark studies involving garlic and natural killer cell function, Dr. Abdullah theorized that if garlic could so dramatically enhance immune function among healthy people, it might be able to help people with compromised immune function, such as victims of acquired immune deficiency syndrome (AIDS). Decreased natural killer cell activity has been established as a poor prognostic factor for patients with AIDS, and efforts to enhance natural killer cell activity may result in varying degrees of improvements for these patients.

In the study, which was reported in the *Journal of Oncology*, Dr. Abdullah gave ten AIDS patients aged garlic extract as a food supplement for twelve weeks. Three of the patients had severe gastrointestinal or neurological problems when the study began, and they were not able to complete the garlic regimen; these three patients died during the twelve weeks of the experiment. Dr. Abdullah, then, was left with seven patients who could complete the test and be evaluated for possible immune system improvement.

During the time they took garlic, the patients noticed improvement in a number of symptoms related to immune suppression of AIDS, including improvement in diarrhea, candidiasis of the mouth and throat, and pansinusitis, plus interruption of the recurrent cycles of genital herpes. Interestingly, the patient who suffered from pansinusitis received relief from aged garlic extract after his symptoms had not responded in more than a year of antibiotic treatment.

There was also significant improvement in

the patients' immune function. Within six weeks, the natural killer cell activity of five of the seven patients was within the normal range; by the end of the twelve-week experiment, all patients had natural killer cell activity within the normal range. The helper/suppressor cell ratio, one of the important indicators of immune status in AIDS, reverted to normal in three patients, improved in two others, and remained normal in one. The platelet count of one patient more than doubled during the period of the study; researchers were fascinated by this development, since low platelet count in AIDS patients has traditionally been resistant to all forms of therapy.

In discussing why the extract had such a dramatic impact on the AIDS patients, researchers have several theories. First, as discussed earlier in this chapter, garlic can stimulate natural killer cell activity, can stimulate macrophage activity, and can modulate the response of T lymphocytes to lymphokines and mitogens. These effects combined may have improved the health of the AIDS patients.

Garlic may also kill many of the opportunistic infections—such as cytomegalovirus, salmonella, histoplasma, and Candida—common to AIDS patients. One study in China recently showed that garlic was extremely potent in reducing both illness and death from cytomegalovirus among bone marrow transplant recipients. Dr. Abdullah himself theorizes that garlic may be effective against the human immunodeficiency virus (HIV), the virus that causes

AIDS. For, as Dr. Abdullah pointed out, "Garlic kills a broad spectrum of disease-carrying organisms—from viruses to bacteria to protozoa."

Dr. Abdullah's study, though limited in size, presents a challenge for further AIDS studies utilizing aged garlic extract and involving wider populations—and may hold promise for the future of AIDS treatment.

CHAPTER FIVE
Garlic and Your Heart

Approximately one out of every two people in the world's industrialized nations will die of cardiovascular disease—diseases of the heart and circulatory system. Almost half as many people die from heart disease as from all other causes of death combined. Heart disease is the number-one killer—and the most expensive illness in terms of health dollars—in the United States, Great Britain and other industrialized nations.

A leading factor in deaths due to heart disease is coronary occlusion, or obstruction of the coronary arteries. Very simply put, the arteries that lead to the heart—the vessels that transport nutrients and oxygen to the heart muscle—get clogged with fatty deposits called plaque. Blood can't circulate effectively to the heart. Eventually, part of the heart muscle dies. The medical name for the resulting condition is myocardial infarction: heart attack. If enough of the heart muscle dies, the heart can no longer function, and death occurs.

A similar physiological process leads to a second major circulatory system killer; stroke. When levels of fat and cholesterol in the blood are high, the blood vessels that form an intricate network through the brain become choked with plaque. As arteries become progressively more narrow, less blood is able to circulate through the brain. Eventually, the artery closes off completely, and part of the brain tissue is deprived of nutrients and oxygen. The result is stroke—death of part of the brain tissue. Depending on how much of the brain tissue is affected, paralysis or death can occur.

Science has established two major risk factors for heart disease. One is high blood pressure, a condition in which blood circulates through the vessels with increased pressure, weakening the blood vessel walls. The other general risk factor is a high level of blood cholesterol, the yellowish, waxy, fatty substance that becomes deposited along the walls of the arteries and eventually leads to plaque buildup.

There are three general sources of cholesterol in the blood. One is dietary: consumption of foods high in saturated fats and cholesterol (those of animal origin) tends to increase the level of cholesterol in the blood, and is responsible for approximately 20 percent of the total blood cholesterol. Whole milk, cream, butter, high-fat cheeses and red meats are particularly high in saturated fats. The higher the fat content of the food, the more fats are absorbed into the bloodstream; fats that cannot be used by your body are stored in the tissues, and eventually spill over into the blood. I advocate a diet high in fiber, vegetable oils such as olive, Canola and peanut oil, and fish oils and low in saturated fats as a front-line defense against heart disease.

A second and often overlooked source of blood cholesterol is your body itself. Endogenous cholesterogenesis, or the manufacture of cholesterol by body cells, is the source of more than 70 percent of the cholesterol in the bloodstream. Body cells produce some fats, but most are produced by the liver. Cholesterol manufactured by body cells is then released into your bloodstream.

A third cause of increased cholesterol in the bloodstream is a dysfunction of your body's normal fat transport mechanism. When your body is working as it should, certain types of fats are routinely transported in the blood from one tissue to another or removed from your body. In some cases, for reasons not entirely understood, a tissue won't "receive" the fats. As a result, they accumulate in your bloodstream after being moved out of a tissue.

Interestingly, some foods that do not contain cholesterol themselves—such as alcohol—nonetheless increase the body's cholesterol load by stimulating endogenous cholesterogenesis and by causing a dysfunction of your body's fat transport mechanisms.

Scientists searching for ways to reduce heart

disease risk have started to look at general population trends, and some fascinating results have surfaced. In one study, researchers found that Asians in Britain run a 50 percent greater chance of suffering from heart disease than Asians who stay in their native land. Why? After analyzing all the factors, researchers believe that much of the increase in heart disease among the migrating Asians is because of dietary changes, including abandonment of their tradition of eating garlic every day.

These and other findings have prompted scientists to take an in-depth look at garlic. Results of intensive research by international teams of scientists show that garlic is effective in lowering blood cholesterol, reducing the level of other fats in the blood, reducing the tendency of the blood to clot, and preventing coronary artery disease.

GARLIC: A TWOFOLD ATTACK ON CHOLESTEROL

Scientists working on ways to reduce cholesterol—and thus the risk of cardiovascular disease—have only recently confirmed what some Mideastern and Oriental cultures have known for many years: regular use of garlic definitely lowers the level of cholesterol in the blood.

Aggressive research shows that garlic effectively reduces the blood cholesterol levels in two ways. First, it slows down *endogenous cholesterol synthesis*, your body's own manufacture of cholesterol. Including garlic in your diet along with reducing calories could, then, help lower cholesterol. Second, it helps your body transport fats from the tissues where they are stored to the bloodstream, which enables them to be eliminated from your body.

The effects of garlic on blood lipids was probably first noted in an epidemiological study of the Jain sect in India, a traditionally vegetarian community whose members often eat large amounts of garlic and onions. Researchers picked people who were similar in age, weight, and social status for the study. The subjects were then divided into three groups, based on their dietary habits: those who ate garlic and onions in liberal amounts, those who ate garlic and onions in small amounts, and those who did not eat garlic and onions at all.

Researchers then compared the cholesterol and triglyceride levels of the three groups. Those who ate garlic and onions liberally averaged 25 percent lower in cholesterol levels than those who abstained. Those who ate liberal amounts of garlic and onions had an average of half the triglycerides of those who didn't eat garlic and onions.

Subsequent studies have confirmed what scientists observed in India. In a study reported in the *American Journal of Clinical Nutrition*, a group of 62 coronary heart disease patients was divided in half. One group served as a control; the other group was given garlic oil on a daily basis for ten months. According to the researchers, the lipoprotein levels remained fairly constant among members of the control group. But those who took garlic enjoyed a steady decrease in low-density lipoproteins and a progressive increase in high-density lipoproteins.

A number of studies show that garlic does indeed reduce the level of fats in the blood. Several animal studies reported in the *Journal of Nutrition* show that various components of garlic keep the liver from manufacturing its own cholesterol.

In one, one group of rats was fed a regular laboratory diet for two months, and a second group of rats was fed the regular laboratory diet supplemented with garlic extract. At the end of two months, the rats whose diets were supplemented with garlic extract had significantly lower levels of lipids (including cholesterol) in the blood as well as fewer lipids in their tissues and less cholesterol and triglycerides in their livers.

In a separate study involving rats, the animals were divided into three groups. The first group was fed a cholesterol-free diet. The second group of rats was fed a diet high in cholesterol. And the third group was fed a high-cholesterol diet supplemented with garlic.

The high-cholesterol diet was shown to affect both high- and low-density lipoproteins. High-density lipoproteins (HDL) carry excess cholesterol to the liver, where it is metabolized; they *protect against* heart disease and stroke. Low-density lipoproteins (LDL) carry cholesterol to the organs and tissues of the body; they *contribute to the risk of* heart disease and stroke.

When the rats ate a diet high in cholesterol, the low-density lipoproteins—*those that increase heart disease*—rose. The high-density lipoproteins—*those that protect against heart disease*—decreased. Simply stated, the animals were at greater risk of heart disease.

What happened to the rats who ate a high-cholesterol diet that was supplemented with garlic? Their levels of low- and high-density lipoproteins were nearly identical to those of the rats who ate a cholesterol-free diet.

Follow-up studies involving both rats and rabbits measured the effect of garlic on diets high in cholesterol and sucrose (common table sugar). Because excessive sugar is broken down into starting materials for the synthesis of cholesterol and other fats, diets high in sugar can increase the amount of cholesterol and triglycerides in the blood. When either high-cholesterol or high-sucrose diets were supplemented with garlic, the animals did not suffer the expected increase in blood fats.

In several studies, researchers deliberately fed rabbits high-fat diets to cause atherosclerosis in the animals. Scientists examined the rabbits and "graded" their atherosclerotic lesions to determine how severe they were. It took only a few weeks of consistently eating garlic to reverse the atherosclerosis in the rabbits. Even rabbits that continued to eat a high-cholesterol diet had a reversal of atherosclerosis if the diet was supplemented with garlic. While these studies show promise for the same effect in humans, they have not yet been duplicated on humans, partly because of the obvious difficulty in designing such a study.

Apparently the impact of garlic on cholesterol and blood fats varies depending on the type of garlic preparation that is used. One study that accurately measured the differences between various garlic preparations was conducted at the University of Wisconsin's Department of Nutrition and was reported at the 1991 National Conference on Cholesterol and High Blood Pressure, sponsored by the National Institutes of Health. Researcher Dr. Asaf A. Qureshi and her colleagues supplemented the corn-based feed for chicks with either garlic powder, garlic oil, Kyolic Aged Garlic Extract, or S-allyl cysteine (a water-soluble component in aged garlic). The chicks were given the enriched feed for a period of four weeks, after which measurements were made of cholesterol, triglycerides and various lipoproteins.

The scientists involved in the study determined that garlic powder had a slight effect in lowering cholesterol; commercial garlic oil did a little better. But the chickens who showed the greatest drop in cholesterol were the ones that ate aged garlic extract. The extract was most effective, followed by garlic oil and, least effective, garlic powder. Even at very low dosages (15 to 405 parts per million in the diet), S-allyl cysteine also had a better effect than garlic oil or garlic powder.

Chickens aren't the only ones who benefit. The study, says Dr. Qureshi, shows that aged garlic extract "may be an effective natural product or food for lowering cholesterol and triglycerides in humans.''

Commenting further on the study, Dr. Qureshi's colleagues told members of the First World Congress (see Appendix A) that the extract may not only lower cholesterol and triglycerides in humans, but may also help prevent the onset of thrombosis.

In a study conducted in China, almost 300 patients with diagnosed high blood lipids were given garlic oil every day for a month, but were not permitted to change dietary habits. At the end of one month, the patients showed a significant drop in cholesterol and a dramatic decrease in triglycerides. In addition, levels of low-density lipoproteins dropped, while levels of high-density lipoproteins increased.

An article published in the *British Journal of Clinical Pharmacology* reviewed eighteen studies in which researchers measured the effects of either garlic or onions on cholesterol. Garlic was consistently shown to reduce cholesterol levels in the bloodstream.

One of the studies examined in the article was conducted by Dr. Benjamin Lau at California's Loma Linda University School of Medicine and was originally published in *Nutrition Research*. In the study, researchers gave people aged garlic extract for a period of six months and determined how the garlic affected blood fat levels.

In the first part of the three-part study, 32 people with high cholesterol were randomly divided into two groups. The first group was given four daily capsules of liquid aged garlic extract. The second was given a placebo (four capsules of a caramel-colored liquid indistinguishable from the extract). Levels of blood lipids (fatty deposits) were measured once a month during the six months of the study.

During the first two months of the study, there was no significant change among those taking the placebo. Not so with the garlic extract group; their blood lipids actually rose slightly during the first two months of the study. Discouraged researchers decided against abandoning the study when they learned that a similar phenomenon had occurred in an earlier study using garlic juice.

By the end of the third month, lipids among those taking aged garlic extract had started to drop. By the end of six months, blood lipid levels had returned to within normal range in 65 percent of the people who took the extract. There was no such drop among those taking the placebo.

Researchers believe that the initial rise in blood lipid levels occurred because garlic moved fats that had been deposited in body tissues to the bloodstream. The result was an initial rise in blood lipid levels, but the garlic eventually helped the fats be metabolized and excreted from the body.

In the second part of the study, researchers considered the impact of garlic on high- and low-density lipoproteins.

When people with high cholesterol levels took aged garlic extract for six months, the levels of HDL (that protect against heart disease) steadily rose. The levels of LDL (that contribute to heart disease) initially rose slightly, but then steadily dropped. "Cholesterol, triglycerides, and low- and very-low-density lipoproteins all dropped, while beneficial high-density lipoproteins rose," said Dr. Lau. "The garlic seems to inhibit the liver's production of harmful blood fats."

The researchers working with Dr. Lau concluded that the extract can significantly reduce dangerous levels of blood cholesterol. One reason, they say, is simple: as Dr. Lau concluded from his study, garlic inhibits the body from manufacturing its own cholesterol. Apparently the sulfur compounds in garlic counteract the biological reaction that produces cholesterol by inhibiting the activity of a key enzyme that initiates cholesterol synthesis.

Dr. Lau pointed out that the effects of garlic can be even more pronounced when accompanied by simple changes in diet. He cited the example of one man in the study who agreed to cut out alcohol for one month. During the month that he cut out alcohol and took Kyolic Aged Garlic Extract, his cholesterol dropped from 320 milligrams per deciliter to 210 mg/dl.

EFFECTS OF GARLIC ON YOUR BLOOD PRESSURE

Hypertension (elevated blood pressure), a significant risk factor for cardiovascular disease and one of the leading causes of atherosclerosis, has become a problem of major proportions in the United States today: experts estimate that one in five Americans suffers from high blood pressure. Drugs are available to control or reduce blood pressure, but most cause moderate to severe side effects.

Garlic has been used in both China and Japan for centuries to control hypertension, which exerts dangerous pressure against blood vessels and weakens arterial walls. Today, pharmacists in Japan recommend an aged garlic extract preparation to their customers with hypertension. This preparation is called Kyo-Leopin, and it is sold as an over-the-counter drug in Japan.

A variety of studies involving animals and humans conducted over the past seven decades show that garlic lowers blood pressure. In one test, laboratory rats were divided into two groups. One group received oral saline (salt solution); the other group received garlic extract by mouth. Over the next five hours, there was no change noted in the blood pressure of the rats who received the salt solution, but the arterial blood pressure of the rats receiving garlic extract was significantly cut. According to researchers, the blood pressure-lowering effects of the garlic extract lasted for 24 to 48 hours.

The same researchers decided to determine whether there were differences between administering an oral dose or injecting the garlic extract. For their experiment, they chose rats with normal blood pressure measurements. When the rats received an injection of garlic extract, blood pressure fell "markedly" and stayed low for approximately 24 hours. When the rats received an oral dose of garlic extract, their blood pressure underwent a slow but sustained drop, with the maximum effect occurring about five hours after they ate the garlic extract.

In a separate study involving 70 dogs, the animals were given injections of garlic extract to determine the effects of the garlic extract on blood pressure. The dogs experienced more than 25 percent reduction in both diastolic and systolic blood pressure after receiving injections of the garlic extract.

Garlic has also been shown to reduce blood pressure in humans. In one study conducted in China, 70 patients with diagnosed hypertension were given garlic oil. Almost half of the patients experienced a "marked" lowering of blood pressure, while fourteen more experienced "moderate" drops in blood pressure.

In a separate Chinese study conducted at the People's Experimental Academy of Health in Zheziang Province, garlic oil was also shown to significantly reduce blood pressure among people with diagnosed high blood pressure.

Apparently the *type* of garlic partly determines how significant the drop in blood pressure will be. In a Bulgarian experiment involving cats, garlic juice resulted in only a "slight and temporary" decrease in blood pressure. But when the juice was aged for up to a year, the blood pressure drop was more significant and sustained. Researchers who conducted the study theorized that aging the juice allowed formation of certain substances that had an effect on blood pressure.

In 1992 a blood pressure-lowering mechanism of garlic was reported in the German scientific journal *Planta Medica*. According to study results, gamma-glutamyl-S-allyl-cysteine, a small peptide in garlic, inhibited the enzyme that catalyzes the conversion of hormones that regulate blood pressure. Angiotensin I does not raise blood pressure; angiotensin II can raise blood pressure. The small peptide in garlic inhibited the enzyme that converts angiotensin I into angiotensin II, therefore lowering the blood pressure.

Because garlic lowers blood pressure, it would seem that people with low blood pressure should avoid garlic in their diets. Just the opposite is true: patients with low blood pressure (hypotension) have actually experienced improvement of blood pressure from taking garlic. Rather than simply *lowering* blood pressure, garlic seems to *normalize* it.

ANTI-CLOTTING PROPERTIES OF GARLIC

Traditionally, Chinese practitioners relied on garlic to promote blood circulation and dissolve clots in blood vessels. Reflecting both traditional practice and sophisticated technology, scientists know that blood clots compromise circulation. In the worst possible scenario, a clot in one of the arteries leading to the heart (a condition called *coronary thrombosis*) results in myocardial infarction, or heart attack.

To understand the beneficial role of garlic, it's important to understand how clots form. Blood clots are made up mostly of *platelets* (small disc-shaped cells), *fibrin* (a mesh-like substance produced when blood coagulates) and trapped red blood cells. A number of studies have shown that patients suffering heart attacks or stroke often have too much fibrin combined with a shortened blood coagulation time—a combination that leads to clots and thrombosis.

Several studies have shown that garlic interrupts the process by which platelets and fibrin work to form clots. Working on the premise that a high-fat diet aggravates fibrin formation and boosts cholesterol, one team of researchers first measured blood fats and fibrinogen in ten healthy adult men. The men were then fed 100 grams of butter (approximately 3½ ounces). Measurements were repeated three hours later. As the researchers expected, there had been a significant increase in blood cholesterol, an increase in fibrinogen, and a decrease in fibrinolytic activity—with the corresponding tendency for the blood to coagulate and clot.

On a separate day, researchers repeated the experiment, this time giving the men garlic extract along with the butter. Three hours later, cholesterol levels remained stable, and fibrinogen levels actually *dropped below normal.* The danger of coagulation and clotting was eliminated.

Garlic and its compounds have been shown in a variety of studies to reduce fibrin formation and to break up existing fibrin. One researcher from George Washington University School of Medicine reported to the First World Congress that he had identified three different constituents of garlic that help prevent platelet aggregation. He concluded that garlic more effectively prevents blood clotting than does aspirin.

The body depends on an intricate system of checks and balances to maintain perfect health. The process of blood clotting provides a perfect example. On the one hand, thromboxane (produced by the platelets) triggers clotting. On the other hand, prostacyclin (prostaglandin I_2 produced by cells lining the blood vessels) guards against clotting. An aqueous extract of garlic has recently been shown to preserve the body's balance by inhibiting the production of thromboxane, but not prostacyclin. A significant decrease in thromboxane B_2 in the blood following the feeding of aged garlic extract has been reported by Dr. Qureshi of the University of Wisconsin.

In Europe, garlic has been used to lower blood lipid levels and to reduce the tendency for the blood to clot, and researchers there believe that it may decrease cardiovascular risk. Garlic is especially popular in Germany, where it is approved as an over-the-counter drug for the prevention of atherosclerosis.

Still another exciting study was conducted by researchers at the University of Wisconsin and was reported to the First World Congress. Researchers used a mechanical device to narrow the coronary arteries, which normally causes platelet aggregation and reduced blood flow. Garlic prevented the platelet aggregations from forming and preserved normal blood flow through the arteries.

In one experiment conducted in Germany, scientists caused platelet aggregation and blood clotting by administering various chemicals known to have these effects, including epinephrine. The researchers then administered garlic extract and measured the results. *Regardless of the clotting agent that was administered,* garlic extract was effective in reducing platelet aggregation and preventing clotting.

In a separate study reported in *Atherosclerosis,* researchers gave garlic to twenty patients with hyperlipoproteinemia, a condition in which there are increased levels of lipoproteins (and, therefore, increased lipid levels) in the blood. During the four weeks in which the garlic was administered, researchers measured blood pressure, serum cholesterol levels, and blood-clotting tendencies. After just four weeks of receiving garlic, all patients enjoyed a 10 percent drop in both systolic and diastolic blood pressure, a 10 percent decrease in serum cholesterol levels, and a 10 percent decrease in the factors that lead to blood clotting and thrombosis.

One garlic compound particularly effective against clotting is *ajoene*, a sulfur compound derived from allicin under certain conditions using heat and organic solvents. Ajoene has been scientifically shown to be as powerful as aspirin in preventing blood clots. It's important to realize that ajoene formation must occur at temperatures well above room temperature, so it is absent from raw or freeze-dried garlic.

In one study conducted at the Venezuelan Institute for Scientific Investigations' Experimental Thrombosis Laboratory, researchers measured the effects of three different components of garlic on the tendency of platelets to clot. While all the components resulted in a decreased tendency of platelets to form, ajoene was four times more potent in preventing platelet formation.

Scientists reporting at the First World Congress said that ajoene is so potent against clotting that it may prove beneficial in various cardiac surgeries, including balloon angioplasty, in which damaged blood vessels are dilated to improve blood flow.

It should be noted, garlic researchers point out, that ajoene is not contained in significant amounts in commercially available garlic products; the ajoene used in scientific experiments is produced from garlic through a specialized process. If commercial garlic products contained significant amounts of ajoene, they could pose a danger to people with hemorrhagic disorders.

BENEFITS OF GARLIC FOR EXISTING HEART DISEASE

A study conducted at India's Tagore Medical College showed that garlic has tremendous benefits even among people with existing heart disease. In fact, the study indicates, it can cut down the risk of having a second heart attack as well as the risk of succumbing to heart disease.

In the study, researchers randomly divided 432 heart disease patients into two groups. The first group was given garlic, and the second group was not; both were followed for three years.

Researchers who reported their findings to the First World Congress said that the garlic made a significant difference: the rate of repeat heart attack among the garlic group was reduced by 30 percent in the second year and by 60 percent in the third year. Mortality rates showed a similar decline: they were reduced by 50 percent during the second year and by 66 percent during the third year among those who took garlic.

Researchers noted with interest that garlic had an even greater effect during the third than the second year. The possible reason, they concluded, is that continuous garlic use progressively reverses atherosclerosis (hardening of the arteries)—and the less the atherosclerosis, the less heart disease and lower risk of heart attack.

Increasing use of sophisticated technology—including infrared spectrophotometry, mass spectroscopy, and high-pressure liquid chromatography—will enable researchers to further define the effective substances in garlic on cardiovascular health. As additional research is completed, investigators may be able to clearly define the exact role garlic can play in the treatment and prevention of cardiovascular disease.

CHAPTER SIX
Treating Cancer

While scientists watched with interest research that demonstrated the effects of garlic on the immune system, a logical question arose: Could garlic's effects on the immune system be powerful enough to mobilize it against a disease as pervasive as cancer? Researchers who saw the antibacterial and antiviral effects of cancer reflected on the possibility that something in garlic could be used to successfully treat certain kinds of cancer.

Research continues, and much more is needed, but studies conducted almost four decades ago indicate that garlic may have cancer-fighting potential on two fronts: it may inhibit tumor growth, and it may mobilize the body's own immune system against the cancer.

INHIBITING TUMOR GROWTH

As early as 1957, researchers who noted the enzyme activity of certain cancers experimented to determine whether components of garlic could affect the oxidation of those enzymes. In a study reported in *Science*, the researchers incubated sarcoma tumor cells with alliinase and the S-ethyl-L-cysteine sulfoxide, then injected the tumor cells into mice. According to the researchers, tumor growth was completely inhibited—and the mice survived beyond the six-month observation period.

Almost a decade later, Japanese researchers injected garlic extracts into rats with ascites sarcoma. The study results, published in *GANN*, showed that garlic has a twofold effect on the cancer: the garlic extracts caused irregularities and scattering of chromosomes in the cancer cells, and the garlic extracts blocked the tumor cells from dividing.

In 1973, a Japanese researcher treated a variety of tumor cell types with fresh garlic extract, then injected the tumor cells into mice. According to the results published in the *Japanese Journal of Hygiene*, tumor development in the mice was "reversed." The same researcher was successful in inhibiting mammary tumors and other sarcomas with a solution of fresh garlic extract.

In research conducted during the last decade, scientists tested fresh garlic and diallyl trisulfide against more conventional treatments—including 5-fluorouracil (5 FU)—on human gastric cancers. The results of the study, published in *Chung Hua Chung Liu Tsa Chih*, found that fresh garlic had a "marked killing effect" on the gastric cancer cells, and that diallyl trisulfide was stronger than 5-FU against the cancer cells.

More recent research also shows that the route of administration may be important in garlic's potential effectiveness against cancer. In one study, live tumor growth was inhibited by 10 to 25 percent among rats who were fed fresh garlic extract, but liver tumor growth was inhibited 30 to 50 percent among rats who were injected with the fresh garlic extract. In a study conducted by Dr. Benjamin Lau and his colleagues that was mentioned in Chapter Four, researchers tested the effectiveness of garlic extract against murine transitional cell carcinoma, a particularly aggressive form of bladder cancer. Researchers found, as reported in the *Journal of Urology*, that the garlic extract was most effective when injected directly into the bladder.

MOBILIZING IMMUNITY AGAINST CANCER

Research has indicated that garlic may also hold promise as a cancer treatment because of its ability to mobilize the body's own immune system against cancer. The study, reported in *Nature*, involved incubating Ehrlich's carcinoma cells with garlic extract mixed with water, then injecting the treated cancer cells into mice.

The mice involved in the study were randomly divided into two groups: one received injections of the pretreated tumor cells; the other group of mice were injected twice with tumor cells that had not been exposed to garlic. Each group of mice received two injections of tumor cells at seven-day intervals.

Fourteen days after the mice received the second injection, researchers found that the mice who had been injected with the garlic-treated cancer cells had developed "strong immunity" to the tumor cells, and were able to resist the challenge of the tumor cells. The mice who were injected with untreated cancer cells, however, developed malignant ascites.

Reporting on the various cancer treatment studies in the *Asia Pacific Journal of Pharmacology*, Dr. Hiromichi Sumiyoshi and Dr. Michael J. Wargovich of the University of Texas M.D. Anderson Cancer Center conclude that, while more research is needed, the "experimental results suggest the possibility of tumor cell growth controlled by garlic."

CHAPTER SEVEN
Cancer Prevention

One in three people will develop cancer at some time in life; one in five will die from it. Cancer ranks second only to heart disease as the leading cause of death in the United States today. It is projected that by the year 2000, one out of two people in the U.S.A. will have some type of cancer during their lifetime, and that cancer will be the number one killer of Americans.

To date, researchers have not found a cure for cancer, due in part to the fact that its causes are so varied and its forms so numerous. Cancer most often develops when the body is damaged by a carcinogen (cancer-causing substance); researchers believe that most cancers—as many as 80 to 90 percent—are caused by environmental carcinogens, most notably tobacco smoke and dietary factors.

The notion of carcinogens as cancer-causing

agents was first advanced more than two centuries ago by the noted British surgeon Sir Percival Pott. When he noted an unusually high rate of scrotal cancer among London's chimney sweeps, he started searching for the common denominator. That common denominator—chimney soot, which we now recognize as a source of polycyclic hydrocarbons—was probably the first substance to be labeled a carcinogen by medical science.

Chemical carcinogens appear to be a major cause of cancer, but they are only one of many different causes. Another well-established cause of cancer is radiation. Much of what we know about the effects of ionizing radiation on the body we have learned by studying people who have been exposed to it—including not only the survivors of the nuclear bombings at Hiroshima and Nagasaki, but also uranium miners, physicians, dentists, radiologists, nuclear industry personnel, and others who suffer occupational exposure.

Still another cause of cancer is viruses. Scientists know that viruses cause a myriad of cancers in animals, and recent research shows that certain human cancers are also viral in origin. The viruses most suspected of causing cancer are those in the herpes family, best known for causing genital herpes, oral canker sores, and infectious mononucleosis. Cancers known to be caused by viruses include cancers of the cervix and uterus, lymphomas, some cancers of the liver and some leukemias.

Due in part to the five-year Designer Foods

Program sponsored by the National Cancer Institute, garlic is now being scrutinized as a possible key player in the prevention of certain kinds of cancers. But exactly *how* garlic works to prevent cancer is still a matter of theory and debate among the experts. Epidemiological studies, such as the one conducted in China and discussed in greater detail below, provide strong impetus for continued research. And scientific studies have shown that garlic inhibits tumor growth, blocks carcinogens, and enhances the immune system against cancer.

OBSERVATIONS IN CHINA AND ITALY

Some of the most compelling evidence linking garlic to the prevention of cancer came from epidemiological observations among two large populations in Shandong Province in northeastern China. Scientists were fascinated by the fact that residents of Cangshan County ate twenty grams of garlic a day—that stacks up to about seven cloves of garlic every day (in China, cooked garlic is consumed, but very rarely raw garlic)—and enjoyed China's lowest death rate from stomach cancer, approximately three deaths per 100,000. Yet residents of nearby Qixia County, where garlic is rarely consumed, suffered *thirteen times* that death rate from stomach cancer: approximately forty deaths per 100,000.

Furthermore, the U.S. and China conducted collaborative studies in Shandong Province to identify certain dietary factors that decrease the risk of stomach cancer. As reported in *Cancer Research* and *Journal of the National Cancer Institute*, complex dietary studies revealed that a significant reduction in stomach cancer risk was associated with increased consumption of allium vegetables, including garlic and scallions.

Another case-control study of stomach cancer and diet was conducted in Italy. Stomach cancer ranks first in cancer mortality in north central Italy, while rates are comparatively low in the south. Researchers conducted detailed dietary examinations to determine the differences between the areas. The results reported in *International Journal of Cancer* showed inverse associations between cooked garlic consumption and stomach cancer risk.

INHIBITING TUMOR GROWTH

As mentioned in Chapter Six, solid research indicates that garlic has potent antitumor activity. According to researchers, garlic's ability to inhibit tumor growth may be due to the interference of cell metabolism through the inactivation of essential enzymes as well as damage to the actual structure of tumor cells.

The discovery that garlic reduces the size of tumors was first made almost four decades ago by researchers at Western Reserve University, as reported in *Cancer Research*. Those early studies showed that garlic extract prevented the growth of tumors by inactivating some of the compounds in the tumor cells themselves.

Chinese researchers studied the effects of fresh garlic extract, diallyl trisulfide, and several traditional drugs against two types of human gastric cancers in the test tube (a study mentioned briefly in Chapter Six). The researchers found that both the fresh garlic extract and diallyl trisulfide, an oil-soluble compound derived from garlic, were more potent than traditional chemotherapies in killing the cancer cells. Other similar studies showed that garlic rendered the tumor cells nonviable.

In commenting on the studies, Dr. Benjamin Lau and his colleagues at California's Loma Linda University School of Medicine caution that the Chinese study did not measure possible toxicity of the fresh garlic extract. In a report published in *Nutrition Research,* Lau and his colleagues maintain that one subsequent study reported in *Nutrition and Cancer* showed that the fresh garlic extract was as toxic to human lymphocytes (immune system cells) as it was to the tumor cells. His own studies, say Lau, show that the fresh garlic extract is "very toxic," while liquid aged garlic extract is effective against the tumor cells but nontoxic to the immune system cells.

A number of studies have been done in which cancer cells were incubated with various components of garlic, then injected into laboratory animals to determine whether the cells caused cancer. In one study, discussed briefly in Chapter Six, researchers incubated tumor cells with alliinase and S-ethyl-L-cysteine sulfoxide. For the study, 75 mice were injected with the pretreated cancer cells; 75 control mice were injected with cancer cells incubated in saline.

No tumors developed in the mice injected with cancer cells that had been incubated with garlic. In contrast, *all the mice injected with cancer cells not exposed to garlic died within sixteen days.*

The same researchers repeated the experiment, injecting garlic into solid tumors of rats with Murphy-Sturm lymphosarcoma. According to the researchers, garlic caused "complete inhibition of tumor growth." When the researchers injected allicin into the tumors, however, there was only partial (approximately 65 percent) reduction in the size of tumors, but not the complete inhibition that resulted from injection of the water-soluble garlic compounds. A later study reported in *Cancer Research* maintains that allicin is effective only when incubated with tumor cells, but not when injected into existing tumors.

In the Japanese study in which mice were given injections of pretreated cancer cells at seven-day intervals (see Chapter Six), scientists found that tumor cells were "inactivated" after even a short incubation with garlic. Other studies confirm these findings; in one, garlic extract was shown to inhibit the enzyme activity of liver cancer cells, rendering them nonviable.

Lau and his colleagues determined that the *route* of garlic administration may have a dramatic impact on effectiveness in preventing cancer. For their study, Lau and his colleagues chose murine—i.e., occurring in mice—transitional cell carcinoma, a particularly aggressive form, and the most common kind, of bladder cancer. Transitional cell carcinoma involves only the superficial layers of the bladder; the greatest challenge in treating the cancer is due to its extremely high rate of recurrence, as high as 50 percent following chemotherapy and 70 percent following surgery. Transitional cell carcinoma claims approximately 10,000 lives each year in the United States alone.

Traditional therapy in recent years for transitional cell carcinoma included injections of *bacillus Calmette-Guerin* (BCG), a live vaccine derived from a bovine form of tuberculosis. The vaccine significantly cut the rate of recurrence from transitional cell carcinoma—but not without cost. According to reports, the treatment irritated the bladder, often led to system-wide infection, and had a high potential for toxicity. Occasionally, there were even more serious complications stemming from the use of BCG.

According to Lau, the results obtained from using BCG were often inconsistent and disappointing, despite its obvious ability to at least partially treat the cancer. In studying the situation, Lau found that BCG was often given in too high a dose, leading to toxicity, that the drug was often administered by the wrong route (it was most often injected intravenously), and that physicians often waited until the tumors were too large before they tried to treat the patients with BCG.

As an alternate to BCG, some researchers began to use *Corynebacterium parvum* (CP), a killed vaccine. It appeared to be more effective than BCG in stopping the growth of bladder cancer in mice, but it too proved to be inconsistent and disappointing.

Concerned with the side effects and inconsistent results obtained with traditional treatments, Lau and his colleagues decided to test aged garlic extract as a treatment for murine transitional cell carcinoma. Their findings, published in the *Journal of Urology*, showed that the extract most effectively reduced the size of tumors and even eliminated cancer without toxic side effects.

The team of researchers tested the various treatments in mice with murine transitional cell carcinoma. They found that those who received the garlic extract had both the lowest incidence of cancer and the smallest tumor sizes.

The researchers then decided to determine whether the method of administration made a difference. Their findings showed that there *was* a difference that depended on how the treatments were administered: when BCG was injected directly into the bladder, it reduced the size of tumors; injected systemically, it did not affect the tumors. Both CP and aged garlic extract reduced tumor size when they were injected systemically; the reduction was even more dramatic when they were injected directly into the bladder.

In a second similar study conducted by Lau and his colleagues, the injections were repeated five times over a period of six days. The findings were dramatic: the CP and garlic extract were both much more effective in treating the cancer than was the BCG, which is still the traditional form of therapy for transitional cell carcinoma.

But what astonished the researchers most was the microscopic examination of the tumors. What they had assumed to be tumors in the mice who were treated with aged garlic extract was actually scar tissue. No tumor cells remained. "In other words," reported Lau, "five treatments actually cured the cancer." Lau was careful to point out that the cure followed local, not systemic, injection of the extract.

BLOCKING CARCINOGENS

In addition to rendering tumor cells nonviable, garlic apparently works to block the ability of carcinogens to damage tissues and cause cancer. In one study spearheaded by Michael J. Wargovich of the University of Texas M.D. Anderson Cancer Center, scientists wanted to determine whether garlic or any of its constituents could protect the colon from radiation damage. Their interest stemmed from the fact that radiation treatment was often the therapy of choice for colon and other pelvic tumors, even though the radiation therapy often caused extensive damage to the epithelial cells of the colon. According to medical documents, a significant percentage of patients suffered strictures, fistulas, and other chronic injury years after the radiation therapy had ended.

For the study, Wargovich and his colleagues fed the mice diallyl sulfide, a sulfur-containing compound of garlic, three hours before exposing the mice to a single whole-body dose of radiation. When the researchers later examined the mice, they found that the diallyl sulfide had "significantly inhibited" radiation damage to the colon.

In summarizing the study, which was reported in *Cancer Research*, the scientists pointed out that the diallyl sulfide protected the colon only when it was administered *before* the radiation exposure occurred. Diallyl sulfide administered after exposure to the radiation did not protect the mice from colon damage. The researchers also confirmed that the amount of protection was directly related to the dose of diallyl sulfide: the more diallyl sulfide the mice were fed, the greater their protection against damage from the radiation.

Wargovich and his colleagues also conducted one of the most important studies on the prevention of cancer in an analysis of esophageal cancer and diallyl sulfide. In the study, Wargovich and his team of researchers fed laboratory rats diallyl sulfide isolated from garlic. Three hours later, they administered a powerful carcinogen, nitrosomethylbenzylamine, known to cause cancer of the esophagus in their particular strain of rats.

Among the rats who received diallyl sulfide before being administered the carcinogen, there was *no* tumor formation. There was 100 percent prevention of both papillomas and squamous cell carcinoma in the rats' esophaguses.

In other research, scientists studied the ability of garlic to block two-stage carcinogenesis—in other words, to block both a primary carcinogen and a secondary carcinogen that promotes the first one.

For the research, which was reported in *Carcinogenesis*, researchers shaved mice and applied to their skin 7,12-dimethylbenz[a]anthracene (DMBA), a potent carcinogen known to cause skin tumors. They then applied phorbol myristate acetate (PMA) to the area three times a week; PMA is known to promote the carcinogenic activity of DMBA. Thirty minutes after applying PMA, the researchers applied garlic oil directly to the skin. The scientists found that the garlic oil "markedly reduced the incidence and magnitude of skin tumors" in a dose-dependent way: the more garlic oil they applied, the greater the reduction in skin tumors.

More recent research, reported at the Proceedings of the American Association of Cancer Research, showed that ajoene, another constituent of garlic, is also effective in blocking the carcinogenic action of PMA.

In other research reported in *Nutrition and Cancer*, scientists exposed mice to benzo[a]pyrene, known to cause tumors of the stomach.

Among the mice who were fed garlic oil, more than 70 percent did not develop tumors.

Another study reported in *Cancer Research* tested a group of organosulfur compounds found in garlic, onions, leeks, and shallots for the ability to protect against the carcinogenic action of N-nitrosodiethylamine (NDEA). Over an eight-week period, mice were given either the organosulfur compound or cottonseed oil (as a control) ninety-six hours before being fed the NDEA.

Recently, in addition to oil-soluble sulfur-containing compounds, a water-soluble compound, S-allyl cysteine, found in aged garlic extract, has been shown to inhibit carcinogenesis. First, Drs. Michael Wargovich and Hiromichi Sumiyoshi at the University of Texas, M.D. Anderson Cancer Center, reported in *Cancer Research* that S-allyl cysteine significantly blocked the development of colon tumors induced by 1,2-dimethylhydrazine, a potent carcinogen, in mice. Additionally, they found stimulated activity of glutathione S-transferase, a powerful detoxifying enzyme, in the liver and colon of S-allyl cysteine treated mice. Considering the results of the study, they speculated that S-allyl cysteine inhibited chemical carcinogenesis through enhancing detoxification of carcinogens. Furthermore, since S-allyl cysteine is considerably safer than oil-soluble sulfur compounds, they consider that it is a prime candidate for further cancer prevention study.

Another research group, Drs. John Milner

and Harunobu Amagase, at Pennsylvania State University, reported in *Carcinogenesis* the inhibition of the binding of a carcinogen to DNA by S-allyl cysteine. After receiving a diet containing S-allyl cysteine, animals received a carcinogen, DMBA, and DMBA-DNA binding in the mammary glands was examined. S-Allyl cysteine dose-dependently inhibited DMBA-DNA binding, and a decrease of about 90 percent in the binding was observed at the highest dosage—1 milligram per kilogram of diet. They stated that S-allyl cysteine is effective against the development of breast cancer as well as colon cancer.

Among the garlic preparations, aged garlic extract is the one most studied for its cancer preventive activities. Dr. Lau and his colleagues at Loma Linda University reported in *Nutrition and Cancer* that the extract decreased the toxicity of aflatoxins, naturally-occurring toxic and carcinogenic metabolites produced by *Aspergillus flavus* and related fungi. These fungi often grow on peanuts, grains, corn, beans and sweet potatoes. Aged garlic extract inhibited the mutation induced by aflatoxin B_1. Also, it significantly inhibited aflatoxin B_1 binding to DNA.

Dr. Nishino and his colleagues, Kyoto Prefectural University of Medicine, reported in *Oncology* and *The Journal of Cancer* that aged garlic extract and its constituent, a phenolic compound, allixin, inhibited the development of skin tumors induced by a carcinogen, DMBA, and a promoter, 12-O-tetradecanoylphorbol-13-acetate (TPA).

Dr. Milner's group reported a series of breast cancer preventive activities of the garlic extract in *Carcinogenesis*. Feeding a diet fortified with aged garlic extract powder prior to a carcinogen (DMBA) injection dose-dependently inhibited DMBA-DNA binding in the breast tissues. Aged garlic extract powder also significantly inhibited the development of breast cancer induced by DMBA. They also found increased detoxifying enzyme (glutathione S-transferase) activity in the mammary glands and liver. In a follow-up study, they compared cancer preventive activities among different garlic preparations. Fresh garlic preparations did not have any inhibitory activity. Garlic powder was found to inhibit DMBA-DNA binding to almost the same extent as aged garlic extract powder. However, the side effects of garlic powder were unacceptably severe. At the effective dosage, the garlic powder caused significant growth retardation in the laboratory animals. According to the researchers, aged garlic extract is the best form of garlic preparation because it is confirmed to be effective as well as safe.

According to Judith G. Dausch of the National Cancer Institute and Daniel W. Nixon of the American Cancer Society, garlic may work to block carcinogens by preventing them from reaching cell DNA. Due to the organic sulfur compounds in the garlic, say various researchers, garlic can "render major carcinogen chemicals . . . less able to exert a toxic effect."

ENHANCING THE IMMUNE SYSTEM

Aged garlic extract has been shown to strengthen the body's immune system against cancer. As mentioned in Chapter Four, research conducted by scientists in Florida show that garlic significantly enhances the activity of natural killer cells, which directly attack tumor cells. The researchers fed study volunteers garlic for three weeks, and then drew blood samples, which were exposed to cancer cells in the test tube. The natural killer cells of the garlic-eaters destroyed 159 percent more tumor cells than the natural killer cells taken from people who had not eaten the garlic.

Researchers of John Wayne Cancer Institute in Santa Monica, California have confirmed that aged garlic extract enhances tumor cell killing activity of peripheral blood lymphocytes. Furthermore, when the extract was administered together with interleukin-2, the treatment was far more effective than interleukin-2 treatment alone. (See Chapter Four.)

Some of the most effective immune system cells against cancer are the macrophages, and recent Japanese research shows that aged garlic extract stimulates macrophage activity. (See Chapter Four.) In the studies, the researchers cultured cells in a test tube with aged garlic extract; two days later, they injected the cells with carcinogens. The cells that had been cultured with the extract were able to resist damage from the carcinogens.

In the experiments with murine transitional cell carcinoma discussed earlier in this chapter, researchers found that the effectiveness of the garlic against the tumors was due in large part to stimulation of the immune system. When researchers studied the tumors under the microscope, they found that garlic "significantly enhanced" the phagocytic activity of leukocytes and other immune system cells.

Reporting on a variety of studies that show garlic's ability to enhance the immune system, West Virginia University researcher Dr. Donald L. Lamm remarked that the "highly beneficial reduction in tumor growth" that occurs with the use of garlic "suggests that it will prove to be a highly effective form of immunotherapy."

Regardless of *how* garlic works to prevent cancer, wrote authors in the professional journal *Carcinogenesis*, garlic "may make an enormous contribution to the therapy of cancer and AIDS."

CHAPTER EIGHT
Garlic, the "Germ" Fighter

Some of the popular anecdotes about the benefits of garlic have to do with its antimicrobial powers; for many, the mention of garlic against disease brings to mind a wreath of garlic cloves used to ward off the common cold or a gargle of garlic juice to heal a sore throat.

Notions like these probably had their beginnings in traditional Oriental medicine. The Chinese have used garlic soup to treat pneumonia; garlic extract or juice to treat typhoid, paratyphoid, and meningitis; garlic vapors to treat whooping cough; garlic suppositories to treat bacterial, yeast and trichomonial infections of the vagina; and various garlic concoctions to treat dysentery. They have even been known to treat acute appendicitis successfully with garlic poultices applied to the abdomen.

Garlic has been used for hundreds of years in a number of cultures to treat diseases caused by bacteria, viruses, and other microorganisms. The Danish, Irish and Russians used garlic for centuries to treat coughs and colds. Both Russian and British medics used garlic poultices topically and externally during World War I to treat bacterial wound infections and to successfully prevent gangrene.

During the early 1950s scientists in China successfully used two different kinds of garlic treatments against influenza. In the first, the researchers used intramuscular injections of a combination containing garlic; administered every four to six hours, the injections relieved many of the influenza symptoms. The scientists successfully used the same garlic combination in the form of nasal drops to prevent influenza. Researchers in Western nations at almost the same time found garlic and garlic combinations effective in treating the common cold.

Early studies such as these helped establish garlic as a powerful antimicrobial that is effective against bacteria, viruses, protozoa, fungi, and parasites, and helped lay the foundation for sophisticated modern research that verified earlier research.

THE EFFECTIVENESS OF GARLIC AGAINST SPECIFIC MICROBES

It was probably early scientific research combined with the perspective of traditional practice that first led to modern experiments designed to test the efficacy of garlic against specific microorganisms. Teams of scientists working across the globe have confirmed that garlic is effective against a wide array of disease-causing agents.

Bacteria

According to studies reported in the *Journal of the National Medical Association* and *Medical Hypotheses*, garlic has been shown to be a powerful antibiotic against a number of gram-negative, gram-positive, and acid-fast bacteria. Garlic has even been shown to be effective against strains of bacteria that usually resist treatment, including staphylococcus, mycobacteria, salmonella, and the species of Proteus bacteria.

While garlic has been shown to be a potent antibiotic, its greater value in cases of infection and disease is in its ability to strengthen the immune system. According to Dr. Hiromichi Sumiyoshi of the University of Texas M. D. Anderson Cancer Center, even those who have demonstrated garlic's antibiotic powers do not recommend it as a substitute for medicinal antibiotic treatment in case of infection. Instead, he says, aged garlic extract can be used in conjunction with antibiotics to build immunity and assist the body in fighting off infection.

Raw garlic should never be used internally as an antibiotic, Dr. Sumiyoshi adds: the antibiotic effects of raw garlic are due to the oxidative power of allicin—which destroys both disease-causing (pathogenic) and friendly bacteria, as well as healthy tissue. The result, says Dr. Sumiyoshi, is a medical dilemma. "If crushed raw garlic is used at high enough dosages to be an effective antibiotic," he explains, "it does harm to the body. If it is used at low enough dosages to avoid harming the body, crushed raw garlic is not effective as an antibiotic."

Viruses

A pair of neurologists from the Shanghai Second Medical University in the People's Republic of China reported to members of the First World Congress (see Appendix A) that they have been using garlic to treat viral encephalitis for almost three decades. The two pointed out that viral encephalitis is not only difficult to treat with conventional methods but is also extremely difficult to diagnose.

The Chinese researchers based their diagnosis of viral encephalitis on two different factors: clinical findings and laboratory tests. The clinical findings included factors such as a history of viral upper respiratory tract infections and a collection of neurological symptoms. The laboratory tests involved in the diagnoses included electroencephalograms, CT studies, and cerebrospinal fluid studies.

From their almost three decades of experience with viral encephalitis, the researchers conclude that the herpes simplex virus is the most probable cause in the majority of cases, and they say that garlic is their substitute of choice in treating the condition.

Studies conducted in the test tube show that garlic is effective against both the influenza B virus and the herpesvirus hominis type I virus. Researchers at the University of New Mexico School of Medicine and the Albuquerque Veterans Administration Medical Center tested garlic extract against three different viruses in test tubes. The viruses were treated with garlic extract and then subjected to sophisticated laboratory tests to determine how viable the viruses remained after being treated with the garlic. The researchers found that the garlic was not effective against the Coxsackie virus (which causes polio), but that it *was* effective against both the influenza B virus and the herpes simplex virus type I.

A variety of experiments have shown that garlic is especially effective against some influenza viruses. In one study reported in the *Japanese Journal of Infectious Diseases*, researchers fed laboratory mice aged garlic extract. They then introduced influenza viruses into the nasal passages of the mice. The mice that had not been given the extract became ill; those that had were protected against the influenza. The researchers suggested that in the test tube, the garlic was shown to be directly effective against the viruses; in some experiments conducted in the body, on the other hand, part of the effectiveness of the garlic may be due to its effects on the immune system, which then mounts an attack on the viruses, too.

Protozoa

Some of the first evidence of garlic's effectiveness against protozoa was based on practical experience: Dr. Albert Schweitzer used garlic to successfully treat amoebic dysentery among the patients at his African clinics.

According to a number of experiments conducted since then by various teams of researchers, garlic has been shown to be effective against a wide array of protozoal infections, including those caused by toxoplasma, cryptosporidia, isospora, and pneumocystis.

According to a report published in the *Journal of the National Medical Association*, garlic's effectiveness against these protozoal infections may indicate its value as a treatment for victims of acquired immune deficiency syndrome (AIDS), since these protozoal infections are responsible for much of the illness in victims of AIDS and AIDS-related complex. While further research is needed, garlic may have particular application in cases or protozoal infection, the article points out, since drugs that are currently used to treat these infections are extremely toxic and can further compromise the immune system.

Parasites

Traditionally, garlic has been used for centuries for its effectiveness against parasites. In clinical practice, garlic has been used to successfully treat tapeworm, hookworm, and Ascaris infections in both humans and animals.

Chinese practitioners have relied heavily

on various forms of garlic as anthelmintics, or agents used to expel worms. While garlic has been widely used to treat parasitic infections in humans, livestock, poultry, and fish, agricultural scientists have also used it to control some of the parasites that contaminate vegetables.

In one recent study, reported in the *Journal of Ethnopharmacology*, Mexican fish farmers used minced garlic along with ammonium-potassium tartrate in their fish culture tank to rid carp of capillaria worms. When the minced garlic was added to the culture tanks, the farmers were able to get rid of 86 percent of the capillaria infestation.

Fungi

Fungal infections are often some of the most difficult to treat; they usually resist traditional treatment efforts, and many of the drugs available for the treatment of fungal infections are toxic when given at high enough doses to be effective or over a long enough period to successfully treat the infection. Garlic, on the other hand, has been shown to be effective against a variety of fungi, including Candida (discussed in greater detail below), histoplasma, aspergillus, coccidioides, and cryptococci.

Both in vitro (test tube) and in vivo (human or animal) studies have shown that garlic and its constituents are effective against fungal infections. In one study, researchers from the University of New Mexico School of Medicine and the Albuquerque Veterans Administration Medical Center diluted fresh garlic extract and tested it in vitro against several strain of *Cryptococcus neoformans*, a fungus that causes a severe form of meningitis. According to a report the researchers made to members of the First World Congress, the garlic was effective against the fungus.

Researchers from China's Shanghai Second Medical University tested whether the garlic would have the same effectiveness when given to patients with meningitis. Commercial garlic extract was given intravenously to five patients with cryptococcal meningitis. When the physicians later tested the blood for evidence that the infection was being cleared, they found twice as much activity against the fungus as they had before administering the garlic extract; antifungal activity was also detected in the cerebrospinal fluid.

The team of researchers from Shanghai Second Medical University previously mentioned as having studied garlic extract against viral encephalitis also reported to members of the First World Congress that they have been successfully treating cryptococcal meningitis for almost thirty years. In reporting to their colleagues, they detailed twenty case histories in which they had used garlic extract, either alone or in combination with amphotericin B. They singled out two cases in which even large doses of amphotericin B had been effective and in which garlic extract and diallyl trisulfide had successfully treated the meningitis. Furthermore, the researchers concluded that allicin is not effective in treatment of meningitis.

Garlic Against Candida Albicans

Candida albicans is the organism responsible for vaginal monilia or candidiasis (more commonly known as a "yeast infection") and is the cause of candidiasis ("thrush") of the mouth, throat, and esophagus. It has also gained recent notoriety as the culprit behind the widely publicized "yeast syndrome." The syndrome—reported to plague millions of Americans but still a subject of considerable controversy in the medical community—is characterized by chronic fatigue, muscle weakness, depression, short-term memory loss, severe premenstrual syndrome, infertility, vaginitis, a variety of gastrointestinal problems, severe diarrhea, skin irritations, asthma, and a host of food and environmental allergies.

Candida albicans is not a foreign invader: the body normally has controlled numbers of it, usually in the mouth and the gastrointestinal and vaginal tracts. The problem occurs when Candida proliferates. A number of factors may cause such proliferation, the most common including the use of antibiotic medications, the use of oral contraceptives, the use of steroid drugs (especially cortisone), and an inadequate diet. When the above-listed factors destroy "friendly" bacteria in the body, Candida is allowed to proliferate unchecked. The results can be anything from a thrush infection of the mouth or a vaginal infection to a more systemic yeast infection.

As mentioned above, the notion of systemic-wide yeast infection (or the "yeast syndrome," as it is more commonly called) is still a subject of controversy among the nation's medical community. A recent article in the *Washington Post* refers to the "long-standing debate in professional circles over the syndrome, which has little credibility in the mainstream medical community because it has no fixed definition and because research on its presumed causes and characteristics has not been published in the more prestigious medical journals."

A recent editorial in the prestigious *New England Journal of Medicine* acknowledged the controversy surrounding the syndrome. Penned by Dr. John Bennett of the National Institute of Allergy and Infectious Diseases, it stated the "few illnesses have sparked as much hostility between the medical community and a segment of the lay public as the chronic candidiasis syndrome." Bennett concluded that the controversy is bound to continue until "additional scientifically sound studies" determine whether the syndrome actually exists.

In the next issue of the journal, physicians from throughout the United States and Canada deluged the publication with letters claiming that, based on their private practices, the "yeast syndrome" is real. Other researchers, too, claim that the syndrome does, indeed, exist—and the public seems to agree. My friend Tennessee allergist Dr. William G.

Crook wrote a book summarizing his experiences with patients, and *The Yeast Connection* sold almost a million copies. Dr. John Parks Trowbridge, whose pioneering work with Candida led to the best-selling book *The Yeast Syndrome*, claims that the "yeast syndrome" is "sweeping our industrialized world, but most people don't even know they have it." Other researchers agree, claiming that more people are ill with Candida than medical experts have estimated.

One of the problems surrounding the entire controversy is that Candida has stubbornly resisted treatment. Nystatin, one of the antifungal drugs most commonly used to treat Candida infection, was recently found in scientific studies to be no more effective than a placebo. As a result, even those physicians who have recognized the existence of the yeast syndrome have often been frustrated in their attempts to treat it.

Early experiments showed that garlic may have promise in treating an overgrowth of Candida. Researchers crushed raw garlic, which produced the powerful cytocidal allicin, and used it in test tubes against both fungus and yeast. The results were what the early researchers had hoped for: the raw garlic killed the yeast in the test tube.

But repeated experiments demonstrated that allicin did not have the same effects on yeast in the body as it had demonstrated in the test tube. Shanghai Medical University neurologist Yan Cai did years of research showing that garlic is effective against yeast infections, but that its effectiveness is *not* related to allicin—which, because of indiscriminate oxidation, can cause gastrointestinal disorders, anemia, and other toxic effects in the body.

While researchers discovered that raw garlic didn't work against Candida, they found that aged garlic extract *is* extremely effective against the yeast, controlling its growth and eradicating it without any apparent toxic effects. Earlier, simple experiments conducted by researchers at Loma Linda University School of Medicine showed that garlic is effective in controlling the growth of Candida. In the study, Dr. Benjamin Lau and his colleagues isolated and cultured Candida cells in test tubes. They then added garlic extract to the Candida cultures; there was no growth of Candida in the cultures to which garlic extract had been added.

Dr. Lau and his colleagues subsequently completed a landmark study in which laboratory mice were infected with Candida and then divided into two random groups. One of the groups was used as a control and was treated with plain saline; the other group was treated with Kyolic Aged Garlic Extract. Scientists made careful studies of the blood, kidneys, and tissues of the mice to determine the rate of Candida growth throughout the period of the study.

Twenty-four hours after treatment, researchers took blood samples to determine how well the Candida was being cleared from the bloodstream. The control mice were shown to have a Candida colony count of 3,500; the mice who had been treated with the garlic extract had a count of only 400 colonies. At 48 hours after treatment, the saline-treated group still had 1,400 colonies; the mice who had received the extract had blood that was *completely free of Candida.*

As part of the study, which was reported in the *International Clinical Nutrition Review,* Dr. Lau and his colleagues also tested the kidneys of the animals, since Candida tends to colonize in the kidneys. As with the blood studies, the mice who had received the garlic extract showed significantly lower colonization of Candida in the kidneys than did the mice who received only saline.

Still another interesting finding from the study was that the mice who had received aged garlic extract had macrophages (immune system cells) with significantly greater germ-killing activity against the Candida than did the mice who received saline.

In commenting on the study, Dr. Lau reported that the garlic extract "hastened the clearance of *Candida albicans* from the circulation of the animals systemically infected with this organism" and that it also reduced the number of yeast organisms in the kidneys.

Scientists believe there are several reasons why aged garlic extract is effective against Candida. The most important reason has to do with the ability of garlic to enhance the human immune response. Dr. Benjamin Lau and his colleagues at Loma Linda University tested immune response to Candida following treatment with the extract. They found that it enhanced the activity of the neutrophils and the macrophages, white blood cells that are essential in the body's immune response. After treatment with aged garlic extract, these cells were more aggressive and more effective in destroying Candida organisms.

Enhanced immune activity has been repeatedly demonstrated in a variety of studies as the probable reason why garlic is effective against many microorganisms and disease conditions. Not only does garlic work directly against the microorganisms, say the researchers, but it boosts the body's own ability to fight invading cells.

CHAPTER NINE
Garlic, Your Body's Protector

Pollution has become one of the major concerns of the nineties, as environmental groups battle to save a planet beleaguered by the cost of catering to a convenience-happy generation. The ozone layer is corroding, the planet is gradually warming, landfills are overflowing, and the world's waterways are choked with sewage. Even the air we breathe is filled with contaminants that can be traced to the cars we drive and the factories we operate.

No one can argue that pollution is bad for the planet; the evidence surrounds even those isolated in the most rural areas of the nation. But pollution also wreaks havoc on the body. Chemicals and heavy metals in the environment are responsible for a whole range of both specific diseases and nonspecific ailments; they accumulate in adipose tissue, major organs, the blood and the brain; and are particularly devastating to people with weakened immune systems. Health professionals have linked the chemical contaminants common in environmental pollutants to a variety of disorders, including multiple sclerosis, Parkinson's disease, chronic fatigue syndrome, Alzheimer's disease and a variety of cancers.

At no other time in history have the people of the world been so exposed to such a wide variety of pollutants in such high concentrations. Lead is a good example: today, lead is found in batteries, household paint, and the exhaust fumes from automobiles, even in our water supply. Scientific studies involving laboratory testing, autopsies and assays on exhumed bodies show that those in the world today ingest approximately a thousand times more lead than our ancestors did even a few hundred years ago.

We are bombarded with what scientists call *xenobiotics*, chemicals that are foreign to living organisms. If the body is healthy and functioning at its peak, it can generally detoxify and eliminate most of the pollutants without a great deal of perceivable damage. But if the body is compromised in any way, or the exposure to chemical contaminants is significant (either because of dosage levels or the potency of the chemical), illness or death can result.

YOUR LIVER: THE FRONT-LINE DEFENSE

The major detoxifying organ of your body is your liver, and it serves as your body's front-line defense against chemical contaminants and other pollutants. The liver inactivates toxic chemicals with detoxifying enzymes, such as glutathione S-transferase, and with agents that act as "chemical scavengers." The detoxifying enzymes of the liver convert contaminants into water-soluble inactive compounds that can then be easily excreted from the body. Unfortunately, the detoxifying ability of the liver is limited, and contaminants can also cause damage to the liver.

It stands to reason that one of the best protection against chemical contaminants and pollutants, then, is boosting the ability of the liver to do its job and protecting the liver against the resulting damage. Research has shown that garlic can do both for you.

In a number of studies, garlic has been shown to boost overall liver function and to increase the activity of protective enzymes in the liver. In several studies, aged garlic extract has been shown to enhance the liver's ability to produce the detoxifying enzyme glutathione S-transferase.

In addition to improving liver function, garlic has been shown to protect your liver against the damage associated with chemical contaminants and pollutants. A variety of studies conducted on human liver cells (in a laboratory) and on animals show that Kyolic Aged Garlic Extract protects the liver from damage even when it is exposed to extremely toxic chemicals. In one Japanese study that was reported in the *Hiroshima Journal of Medical Sciences*, researchers maintained human liver cells in a tissue culture and then exposed them to the highly toxic chemical carbon tetrachloride, known to cause liver damage. Through a very sophisticated system of testing, the researchers found that four of the six sulfur-containing compounds isolated from the garlic extract protected the liver against the damage.

Other researchers who analyzed the study results attribute garlic's protection to both its sulfur-containing compounds and a host of nutrients found in the garlic extract. Among the most important elements in protecting the liver, say the researchers, are S-allyl cysteine, S-allyl mercaptocysteine, and selenium. Interestingly, all but selenium are also components of the liver's main antioxidant enzymes.

In a separate study involving mice, researchers used toxic chemicals to induce hepatitis in the mice. In their study, which was reported in *Phytotherapy Research*, the scientists then divided the mice into groups and tested a variety of garlic products to determine whether any of the products provided protection against the liver damage that almost certainly accompanies hepatitis. The researchers concluded that the best protection was provided by S-allyl cysteine and S-allyl mercaptocysteine, two major water-soluble sulfur compounds in aged garlic extract. Wakunaga Pharmaceutical Company, manufacturer of Kyolic Aged Garlic Extract, has applied for patents that will enable two of the extract's compounds—S-allyl cysteine and S-allyl mercaptocysteine—to be used as drugs to protect the liver and treat liver disease.

Independent scientists conducting separate research at the Pharmaceutical Institute of Japan's Tohoku University also tested the ability of garlic to protect against liver damage. They isolated various compounds and tested how effective they were against damage induced by carbon tetrachloride and a second potent liver toxin, D-galactosamine. They found that S-allyl mercaptocysteine and S-methyl mercaptocysteine were both effective in protecting the liver from the chemical-induced liver damage, but that alliin didn not provide protection to the liver.

Garlic is also apparently effective not only in preventing liver damage, but also in treating it. According to a scientific report published in the *Japanese Journal of Pharmacology*, carbon tetrachloride causes most of its damage by causing an accumulation of triglycerides in the liver tissue, resulting in "fatty liver." In a Japanese study designed to measure how effective garlic is in treating liver damage, researchers gave mice carbon tetrachloride. After allowing enough time for liver damage to occur, they then fed the mice aged garlic extract. According to the researchers, the garlic extract inhibited the formation of fatty tissue in the liver.

DAMAGE FROM HEAVY METALS

Some of the most prolific contaminants in the environment today are heavy metals, including lead and mercury. As mentioned, lead is found in a number of common objects, such as paint and batteries, with the result that we absorb one thousand times more lead than our ancestors did a century ago. Another example of heavy metal contamination is mercury. It can cause nervous system damage and paralysis; at high enough concentrations, it kills. Yet it is used in dental fillings and is a common contaminant of the fish we eat.

Research has found that the sulfhydryl compounds in garlic bind to heavy metals, rendering them harmless to the body. As reported in a number of professional journals, garlic has been shown to be effective in the treatment of lead, mercury, cadmium, and arsenic poisoning, mainly because it binds to the metals and other toxins and facilitates their excretion. The mechanism of the protection appears to be the sequestering of metals by the sulfhydryl compounds of garlic. Since garlic is rich in these compounds and their precursors, it is particularly effective in providing this protection.

Specific studies have tested the effects of garlic in general and aged garlic extract in particular against heavy metals. In one recent study conducted by Dr. Benjamin Lau at California's Loma Linda University School of Medicine, ten test tubes were each filled with a suspension of human red blood cells. Researchers then put a heavy metal in each of eight test tubes: lead was added to two, mercury to two, copper to two, and aluminum to two. Two test tubes were left alone and were used as controls.

Scientists then added aged garlic extract to one of the tubes containing lead, one containing mercury, one containing copper, one containing aluminum, and one of the controls.

Examination showed that the red blood cells contaminated by heavy metals underwent "lysis"; the membrane of the cells was ruptured or otherwise destroyed, and the contents of the cell escaped. Simply put, the cells were destroyed. In the test tubes containing aged garlic extract, however, lysis did not occur, even in the presence of heavy metal contamination. Researchers reporting on the study in the *International Clinical Nutrition Review* concluded that aged garlic extract protects red blood cells from heavy metal damage.

Other small-scale studies confirm the ability of garlic to protect against heavy metal damage. In one, a dentist practicing in Honolulu, used garlic to treat fourteen dental patients who had been given silver-mercury amalgam dental fillings. His study showed that the garlic aided in detoxification and elimination of the mercury from the patients' systems.

PROTECTION AGAINST IONIZING RADIATION

Exposure to ionizing radiation is more common than many people imagine. While most people associate radiation with atmospheric fallout from nuclear tests or accidents such as the ones that happened at Chernobyl or Three Mile Island, many don't understand that there are other, more common, sources of ionizing radiation. One source, for example, is the radon emissions from granite, a source that scientists and health experts consider to be a major hazard. the effects on the body can be devastating.

Some are also exposed to ionizing radiation in the course of medical screening or treatment, with subsequent deleterious effects. In one study reported in the prestigious *New England Journal of Medicine*, researchers followed up on more than ten thousand people who had received irradiation before the age of sixteen as a treatment for tinea capitas. When compared to more than ten thousand controls matched for gender, age, and country of birth who had not received irradiation, researchers said the study "clearly confirms" that radiation doses used in the treatment "significantly increase the risk" of brain tumors, nerve-sheath tumors, and other neural tumors.

In one landmark study, scientists incubated human lymphocytes (the immune system's white blood cells) in cultures of living tissues that had been removed from the body. Some of these tissues were then infused with fresh garlic, some with L-cysteine, and some with aged garlic extract. Some tissues were not infused with garlic at all. Scientists then irradiated the tissues with 2000 rads; one culture was not exposed to either radiation or garlic.

Scientific examination of the tissues during the three days following irradiation confirmed the protective ability of garlic. The cultures were microscopically examined 3, 24, 48, and 72 hours following irradiation. In the control culture, the one that was exposed to neither garlic nor radiation, the white blood cells stayed viable throughout the entire 3-day period of the study.

In the cultures that *were* exposed to radiation, resulting damage varied depending on what the cells had been cultured in prior to radiation exposure. In the tissues not protected by garlic, white blood cells died almost immediately. In those protected by fresh garlic, most of the white blood cells were destroyed within the first three hours (some by the oxidizing effect of raw garlic); at the end of 24 hours, all the white blood cells in the culture were dead.

The tissues infused with aged garlic extract or L-cysteine, on the other hand, were significantly protected from the damaging effects of the radiation. At the end of the 72-hour test period, approximately 80 percent of the lymphocytes were still alive and viable.

Researchers have concluded from this and other studies that while fresh garlic actually has toxic effects, aged garlic extract appears to protect against radiation damage.

GARLIC AND FREE RADICAL DAMAGE

Free radicals are molecules that carry an extra unpaired electron. A molecule is the smallest complete unit of any chemical; it consists of a collection of atoms that are held together by positively and negatively charged particles (protons and electrons). When the atoms (or electrons) are paired, the molecules act normally. An extra, unpaired electron, on the other hand, becomes highly reactive to the molecules that surround it.

In some cases, the effects of an unpaired electron are beneficial. For example, free radicals are an important part of normal physiological processes, like the electron transport systems (respiratory chain) involving many oxidation and reduction reactions: free radicals help carry electrons and help produce energy—adenosine 5'-triphosphate (ATP). Free radicals are also used by the immune system as chemical "weapons" to attack invaders.

But if there are too many free radicals in the body, or their activity becomes uncontrolled, excessive damage can occur. These wildly thrashing free radicals can generate excessive oxygen (or oxidation) and damage surrounding tissues, resulting in disease. A number of conditions, including cataracts, atherosclerosis, rheumatoid arthritis, liver disease (such as primary biliary cirrhosis and fatty liver), chronic pancreatitis, Parkinson's disease, and even some cancers, have been linked to free radical damage. The potential damage from free radicals poses a particular risk for people who have only one copy of certain genes (if there are two copies of each gene and one is damaged, there is still a "spare").

Free radicals originate from a number of

sources. One is excessive exposure to X-rays. Another is radioactive contamination. Still another is pollution: free radicals are generated from pesticides, industrial solvents, petrochemicals, chlorinated hydrocarbons, heavy metals and other substances. As a result, most people are exposed to free radicals in drinking water, food, air, household solvents, cosmetics, drugs, cigarette smoke and even some toys.

The body, when healthy, has protective mechanisms to protect it against damage from free radicals. If the body is compromised by inadequate nutrition, stress, fatigue, underlying disease, or other problems, it cannot adequately protect itself from free radical damage.

Researchers have found that garlic, rich in sulfhydryl and related compounds, is one of the best protective agents against free radical damage. But they emphasize that free-radical protection does not originate from *fresh* garlic, which causes oxidative damage itself. In one study that differentiated between the effects of raw garlic and other kinds of garlic products, Dr. Robert Lin and his colleagues at the University of California at Irvine mixed raw garlic and a number of other garlic supplements with human blood in test tubes.

When raw garlic was mixed with human blood, the blood turned an almost black color. Analysis of the darkened blood showed that the iron in the blood had oxidized, the apohemoglobin had oxidized, and the red blood cells had become smaller and misshapen. Some of the other garlic products caused a similar darkening of the blood, with similar microscopic findings. But the blood that had been mixed with Kyolic Aged Garlic Extract was protected from oxidation damage; microscopic examinations confirmed that the blood had not been oxidized.

Dr. Toshiaru Horie and his colleagues reported in *Planta Medica* the protection of liver microsomal membrane from lipid peroxidation by aged garlic extract. The liver microsome, with and without the addition of the extract, was incubated in a mixture of ascorbic acid and ferrous sulfate, which can generate free radicals and oxidize lipids in the membranes of the microsome. After the incubation, they determined lipid peroxidation. The results showed that the garlic extract dose-dependently inhibited lipid peroxidation and served to maintain membrane fluidity (peroxidation of lipids in the membrane results in loss of fluidity). In a subsequent study, they found that sulfur-containing compounds were responsible for inhibiting the lipid peroxidation.

The ability of garlic to protect against free radical damage is directly related to its ability to protect against radiation, which was discussed in greater detail above. Preliminary results from various studies also show that garlic may well protect against the free radical damage that causes premature aging and a number of degenerative diseases, including cancer.

The role of garlic as a preventive against damage to the body appears to be potentially vast. Based on a number of studies conducted by research teams from throughout the world, scientists have concluded that part of the preventive effect of garlic against cancer is due to protection against free radical damage. But that protection extends beyond the mere ability to protect against disease. The ability of garlic to protect against free radical damage may have yet another important benefit to cancer victims: it can, according to several published articles, protect against the damage that results from radiation treatment and chemotherapy commonly given to many cancer patients.

APPENDIX A
The First World Congress on the Health Significance of Garlic and Garlic Constituents

In a landmark three-day event that gathered scientists from fifteen nations, the First World Congress on the Health Significance of Garlic and Garlic Constituents was held in Washington, D.C., August 28-30, 1990. Cosponsored by the Pennsylvania State University, the United States Department of Agriculture, and Nutrition International, the Congress featured forty-six presentations by more than fifty scientists who met to share their most current findings on how garlic protects health. I was fortunate enough to attend this conference.

A number of presentations focused on the various medicinal and pharmacological properties of garlic, including its effect against specific organisms. While the antibacterial properties of garlic have been widely accepted for years, scientists reporting at the First World Congress provided proof that garlic is also effective against viruses, protozoa, parasites, fungi, and yeast.

One microbiologist from the University of Kuwait described research showing the effect of garlic against *Candida albicans*, a common yeast responsible for a variety of syndromes, including vaginal yeast infections. According to Dr. Mahmoud A. Ghannoum, garlic extract weakens the structure of the cell walls, alters the contents of the yeast organism and reduces its ability to adhere to body cells and tissues.

Ghannoum is currently conducting research to determine whether garlic extract can be effective in the treatment of intestinal *Candida albicans* infections in humans. If his research is positive, he and others at the First World Congress predict a major impact in the eventual use of garlic in treating a number of conditions, including chronic fatigue syndrome, the highly controversial yeast syndrome, and a number of persistent opportunistic infections associated with AIDS and AIDS-related complex.

The majority of researchers at the conference, however, addressed the effect of garlic in preventing cardiovascular disease and cancer, two major killers in the world's industrialized nations. It was indeed an historic meeting of experts from around the world.

CARDIOVASCULAR DISEASE PREVENTION

Dr. Robert I. Lin, who chaired the First World Congress, began the scientific meeting by presenting the nutritional and pharmacological properties of garlic. One of the primary effects he discussed was the ability of garlic to lower blood cholesterol levels.

A number of the other scientists reporting at the First World Congress confirmed the cholesterol-lowering ability of garlic. David Kritchevsky of Philadelphia's Wistar Institute of Anatomy and Biology pointed out that garlic has been proven to lower cholesterol levels in both animals and humans. And while garlic reduces levels of low-density and very-low-density lipoproteins (the dangerous kind of cholesterol), Kritchevsky showed that it also raises high-density lipoproteins, those that protect against cardiovascular disease.

The overall effect, said Kritchevsky, is that garlic is effective in inhibiting atherosclerosis, a major form of cardiovascular disease.

In two separate presentations, a team of researchers headed by Dr. Qureshi reported the result of studies showing that aged garlic extract lowers cholesterol and triglycerides in the blood. Qureshi and her colleagues used Kyolic Aged Garlic Extract in the experiments, which caused a "drastic" reduction in low-density lipoproteins among chickens that were fed a diet high in fats. In commenting on the study, Dr. Lin remarked that Kyolic "may be an effective natural product or food constituent" for lowering cholesterol, and that it may "prevent and control the development of atherosclerosis in humans."

Other researchers reporting at the First World Congress showed that various garlic preparations reduce platelet aggregation and reduce thrombosis, important factors in preventing cardiovascular disease.

CANCER PREVENTION

Information on cancer prevention and garlic presented at the First World Congress centered around an ongoing $20.5 million five-year study undertaken by the National Cancer Institute. The so-called "Designer Foods Program" (which is discussed in Chapter One) is assessing the effect of certain vegetables—such as garlic, onions, and leeks—on cancer treatment and prevention.

According to Dr. Herbert F. Pierson, the National Cancer Institute scientist who is directing the study, of all the vegetables being studied, "garlic is the best candidate as a cancer-fighting substance." Pierson chaired the session of the First World Congress in which ten scientists presented their findings regarding garlic and cancer prevention. He also gave his own address on the role of garlic in cancer prevention.

Several different teams of researchers reporting at the First World Congress described test results showing that aged garlic extract prevents cancer in animals that have been given powerful carcinogens known to cause cancer. In two separate studies reported at the First World Congress, aged garlic extract was effective in preventing cancer of the colon in mice.

In another study, Michael J. Wargovich and his colleagues at the University of Texas M.D. Anderson Cancer Center gave mice a carcinogen that causes cancer of the esophagus. Diallyl sulfide, one of the main principles in garlic, was completely effective in preventing cancer of the esophagus. Wargovich says that the study results "may lead to useful avenues of cancer control in man."

THE ALLICIN CONTROVERSY

Central to the First World Congress was discussion of the safety of garlic and the controversy surrounding allicin. Researchers stressed the safety problems connected with the use of raw garlic, especially when taken in large doses. In addition to causing contact dermatitis, said the scientists who reported their findings, raw garlic can cause gastrointestinal irritation, peptic ulcer, diarrhea, anemia and growth retardation. University of Texas researcher Osamu Imada emphasized that the same effects are produced by allicin, a constituent of garlic abundant in raw garlic juice.

Dr. Imada stressed that the only available commercial garlic preparation that has been confirmed safe in toxicological studies is aged garlic extract, a form of garlic that contains no allicin. Aged garlic extract is safer than raw garlic or other commercial garlic preparations because the aging process almost completely eliminates the toxins associated with allicin decomposition, Dr. Imada told members of the First World Congress. It is also more effective than other products because the aging process enhances the compounds in garlic that are responsible for its nutritional and pharmacological properties—particularly the thiallyl compounds, such as S-allyl cysteine.

Tokyo College of Pharmacy researcher Toshiharu Horie reported on research that further enhances the safety issue surrounding aged garlic extract. Dr. Horie's research proved that aged garlic extract protected the liver and other membranes from "peroxidation," a process closely related to toxicity, disease, and aging.

Because of its safety and effectiveness, aged garlic extract is being used in an increasing number of studies involving garlic. Of the 46 presentations at the First World Congress, 14 involved the use of Kyolic Aged Garlic Extract.

As chairman of the First World Congress, Dr. Lin expressed concern that some garlic manufacturers have marketed their products with allicin claims.

"Allicin is a transient and highly unstable compound, and no garlic product contains detectable amounts of allicin," Dr. Lin emphasized to Congress participants. "There is no evidence showing that allicin is the active compound in garlic." According to Dr. Lin, a number of studies, including those presented at the First World Congress, show that the nutritional and pharmacological properties of garlic are due to other compounds in the herb, not to allicin.

"The claim that allicin is the only active principle of garlic is unfounded," Dr. Lin concluded, "rather, it has little direct contribution to garlic's nutritional/pharmacological properties. Excessive consumption of allicin may cause toxicity."

According to Dr. Lin, findings of the researchers gathered for the First World Congress can be summarized as follows:

- Garlic in its various forms—including raw garlic juice, cooked garlic, garlic oil, garlic powder, and aged garlic extract—provides health benefits.
- Increased garlic intake can reduce potential damage from oxidation, free radicals, and nuclear radiation.
- Certain levels of garlic intake can reduce the cardiovascular and cancer risks of populations with modern industrialized lifestyles.
- Since cardiovascular disease and cancer together constitute the overwhelming number of deaths in industrialized nations, it is recommended that people living in these nations increase their consumption of garlic (and/or garlic products) to an average of a few grams per day per person.

APPENDIX B
Garlic Colloquium/Europe 1991

Following up on research presented to more than 250 participants at the First World Congress on the Health Significance of Garlic and Garlic Constituents, some of the world's leading garlic scientists gave presentations in three major cities as part of Garlic Colloquium/Europe 1991. The colloquium featured presentations in Amsterdam, Holland; Copenhagen, Denmark; and Stockholm, Sweden.

Scientists presenting information at the colloquium in October 1991 discussed the future of garlic; findings from the First World Congress; the chemistry and pharmacology of garlic; and discussions regarding the toxicity of various garlic preparations. Participants at the colloquium also heard updated evidence that garlic is effective in preventing cancer, preventing cardiovascular disease, and enhancing human immunity.

Dr. R. P. Labadie, a professor of pharmacognosy at Holland's Utrecht University, kicked off the colloquium by predicting that garlic has a promising future. Dr. Labadie, whose research activities have focused on the phytochemical and chemotaxonomical aspects of plants and the synthesis of plant substances, predicted to audiences that garlic will become an important dietary constituent worldwide and will be recommended by governments for its ability to prevent cancer and cardiovascular disease.

In a summary of the First World Congress presented a year earlier in Washington, D.C., Dr. Raimo Hiltunen focused on research that outlined garlic's ability to prevent cancer and cardiovascular disease. A professor of pharmacognosy at Finland's University of Helsinki, Dr. Hiltunen has been affiliated with Finland's Institute for Forest Research, the Biochemical Research Institute, and the State Natural Science Commission. His research has focused on the chemical analysis of medicinal plants, and he has published more than three hundred articles relating to medicinal plants and their effects. For his contributions to the advancement of chromatography, Dr. Hiltunen received a citation from the Academy of Sciences in the former Soviet Union.

With 25 percent of the First World Congress presentations focusing on garlic and cancer prevention, Dr. Hiltunen centered his remarks on the effectiveness of Kyolic Aged Garlic Extract in protecting against carcinogens. He told colloquium attendees that the commercial garlic preparation has been proved effective in decreasing the risk of stomach cancer; in preventing breast cancer; in suppressing skin cancer growth; and in treating cancer of the bladder.

Dr. Benjamin Lau, a professor of microbiology and surgery at California's Loma Linda University School of Medicine, provided members of the colloquium with an update on garlic research. Recipient of the Basic Science Educator Award of 1991, Dr. Lau has also received numerous awards for his research on cancer immunology. His cancer studies have focused on prevention and natural immunity as a way of reducing deaths from cancer.

In his colloquium presentation, Dr. Lau reported that the latest research shows that garlic can enhance the body's defense ability against pathogenic microorganisms and cancer cells. The research also shows that garlic helps living cells excrete toxic substances that have been known to cause cancer. Other leading research conducted since the conclusion of the First World Congress, Dr. Lau reported, confirmed the ability of garlic to minimize *Candida albicans infections*.

Additional information about the ability of garlic to prevent cancer was presented to the colloquium by Dr. Hiromichi Sumiyoshi, a research scientist at the University of Texas M. D. Anderson Cancer Center. He told members of the colloquium that the development of cancer begins with nuclear damage to the cells—damage that can be effectively prevented by the S-allyl cysteine in garlic.

An accomplished oncologist who specializes in cancer prevention, Dr. Sumiyoshi has focused his research on the ways in which garlic's organosulfur compounds protect against gastrointestinal cancers. Prior to his work at the M. D. Anderson Cancer Center, he conducted research at the Hiroshima University School of Medicine.

Dr. Robert I. Lin, who chaired the First World Congress, presented a comprehensive look at the chemistry and pharmacology of garlic's active principles to members of Garlic Colloquium/Europe 1991. In his presentation, he pointed out how vastly garlic differs from most other vegetables and herbs due to the presence of thioallyl compounds. Those compounds, he reported, are mainly responsible for the nutritional and pharmacological properties of garlic.

Index

Abdullah, T., 41, 50–52
acquired immune deficiency syndrome (AIDS), 50–52, 92, 98, 121
ajoene, 70
allicin, 13, 26, 103
  controversy, 18–22, 124–126
alliinase, 19
Allium sativum, 2
Amagase, H., 89
amino acids in garlic, 14–15
Ascaris infections, 98
atherosclerosis, 69

bacterial infections, 93, 95–96
Bennett, J., 102
Block, E., 11, 32

blood pressure, 63–66
Brewer, W. R., 18

cancer prevention, treatment, 9–10, 77–92, 123–124, 129
Candida albicans, 101–106, 121, 129
carbohydrates in garlic, 15
carcinogens, 78, 85–90
Cavallito, C., 12
China, research in, 79–80
cholesterol, 54–63
Crook, W., 103

Dausch, J. G., 90
Designer Foods Program, 7–8, 78–79
dysentery, 93, 98

131

enzymes in garlic, 15

First World Congress on the Health Significance of Garlic and Garlic Constituents, 21, 35, 61, 70, 71, 120–126
Four Thieves' Vinegar, 6, 31
free radical damage, 115–119
fungi, 99–101

gangrene, 94
garlic
    aged extract, 31–32, 52, 89–92, 96–97; *see also* Kyolic
    ajoene in, 70
    allicin in, 13, 26, 103, 18–22, 124–126
    alliinase in, 19
    amino acids in, 14–15
    anti-clotting, 66–70
    bacteria and, 95–96
    blood pressure and, 63–66
    cancer prevention and, 77–92, 85–90, 123–124, 129
    cancer treatment, 73–75
    Candida albicans and, 101–106, 121, 129
    carbohydrates in, 15
    Chinese uses of, 93
    cholesterol and, 56–63

    commercial products, 23–37
    constituents of, 3, 12–23, 26, 32–34, 70, 103, 110, 124–125, 129–130
    cooked, 26–29
    enzymes in, 15
    free radicals and, 115–119
    fresh juice, 26–29, 81
    fungi and, 99–101
    heart disease and, 53–76, 122–123
    heavy metals and, 111–113
    history of, 1–10
    immune system and, 38–52, 91–92
    ionizing radiation, effects on, 113–115
    meningitis and, 100
    minerals in, 16
    nucleic acids in, 17
    oils, 30–31, 60
    parasites and, 98–99
    powders, 29–30, 60
    products, standardization of, 25
    protozoa and, 98
    raw, 26–29; toxicity of, 21, 81; adverse effects of, 95–96; anemia and, 28; indigestion and, 28; raw ineffective against *Candida albicans*, 104
    supplementation, 126
    toxicity of, 21, 35–36, 81

tumor growth and, 80–85
various uses (poultice, drops, suppository, injections), 93–94
vitamins in, 16
Garlic Colloquium/Europe, 1991, 127–130
Ghannoum, M., 121

HDL cholesterol, 58
heart disease, 53–76, 122–123
herpes simplex I, 97
Hiltunen, R., 128
hookworm, 98
Horie, T., 125
hypertension, 63–66

Imada, O., 124–125
immune system, 38–52, 91–92
influenza, 94
Irie, R., 42–43
Italy, research, 79

Kyo-Leopin, 64
Kyolic Aged Garlic Extract, 10, 32–34, 46–49, 60, 63, 109, 118, 125, 128

L-cysteine, 114–115
Labadie, R. P., 128
Lau, B., 43, 62, 75, 81–85, 112, 129
LDL cholesterol, 58

lead, 111–113
Lin, R. I., 19, 21–22, 24–25, 36, 122, 125–126
liver function, 108–111

meningitis, 93, 100
mercury, 111–113
Milner, J., 88
minerals in garlic, 16

Nixon, D. W., 90
nucleic acids in garlic, 17
Nystatin, 103

parasites, 98–99
Pasteur, L., 6
Pierson, H., 8, 123
pneumonia, 93
polio virus, 97
Pott, P., 78
protozoa, 98

Quereshi, A., 60, 68, 122

radiation, 78, 113

S-allyl cysteine (SAC), 34, 88, 110
Schnell, E., 32
Schweitzer, A., 1, 7, 98
Seebeck, E., 13
Semmler, F. W., 12
Stoll, A., 13

Sumiyoshi, H., 76, 88, 95, 129

tapeworm, 98
trichomonial infections, 93
Trowbridge, J., 103
tumor growth, 73–75, 80–85
typhoid fever, 93

viruses, 96–97
vitamins in garlic, 16

Wargovich, M. J., 76, 85–86, 88, 124
Wertheim, T., 11
whooping cough, 93
worms, intestinal, 4

Yamasaki, Dr., 47